DYLAN THOMAS

DYLAN THOMAS

'Dog Among the Fairies'

By

HENRY TREECE

LONDON
ERNEST BENN LIMITED

First Published 1949
Second Edition (Revised and reset) 1956
Second Impression 1957

Published by Ernest Benn Limited
Bouverie House, Fleet Street, London EC4
Printed in Great Britain

Born Swansea 27 October 1914
Died New York 9 November 1953

'. . . . . . . *a dog among the fairies,*
The atlas-eater with a jaw for news.'

DYLAN THOMAS   25   POEMS

Contents

Introduction

After the funeral, mule praises, brays,
Windshake of sailshaped ears . . .

NOW HE is Dylan to us all. We all share him; the black-coated literary gentleman mouthing *Fern Hill*, the mournful critic who wasn't very kind once below a time, and the old lady in the front row. Dylan to us all, for his death has strangely left us all a little smaller. Although it is as familiar as bread, I shall dare to quote this passage, for it says better than I, or any other writer living, can say, something of what that death means:

> *No man is an island, entire of itself; every man is a*
> *piece of the continent, a part of the main. If a clod*
> *be washed away by the sea, Europe is the less, as well*
> *as if a promontory were, as well as if a manor of thy*
> *friends or of thine own were; any man's death*
> *diminishes me, because I am involved in mankind.*
> *And therefore never send to know for whom the bell*
> *tolls. It tolls for thee.*

The news of his death affected me more strongly than I had thought possible, although I had known him well only for a short period. It was like a vicious and unexpected blow under the heart. How it must have affected those who knew him intimately, I dare not imagine, nor they describe. Though one did not need to know him well to fall under his spell. I know many quite unliterary people, people who hadn't opened a book of poems since their schooldays, if then, to whom Dylan's appearance on Television was a major event. He was, like Kim, 'Little friend of all the world'. Though in his amiably contemptuous way that is the last description he would have allowed.

This attraction which he held is inexplicable. As a poet he was for the most part, as every romantic poet must be, an introvert; yet as a man he was exactly the opposite. He seemed to be unaware of himself except as part of a group —yet a group which always elected him as the Life and Soul of the Party.

I think he had a peculiar sort of honesty which drew friends to him—honesty to craft and to craftiness. With the twenty-two carat trumpet of an Archangel and the glutinous smile of a young boy, he battered and coaxed his admirers no less than his critics into a divine insensibility. In his presence, one's eyes were blinded to the cocky strut of his appearance, one's sense of judgment blunted to his rogueries. One became a willing victim to the superb deftness with which he flung the glittering golden net of his voice; one was caught forever by the rich sounds he made, a minnow in the vocal jamjar of a tangly-haired urchin.

There lay his supreme honesty, that he never pretended he would not trick anyone within earshot! You went into it with your eyes open, and thereafter stayed with them shut—so as better to hear the splendid music of his words. Dylan Thomas was remarkable (apart from being a genius) in that he was a rare example not so much of the Literary Bohemian as of the common-or-garden scallawag, the Young Rip we all envy and wish we could be, but dare not. The enormous majority of us 'grow up', get old and anxious and responsible. We let society hamstring us a hundred ways— making us pay our rent and dig our gardens, economise on tobacco and drink, put on thick underwear when the leaves begin to fall. But Dylan just remained himself, his honest scallywag self, and was inevitably destroyed, like all other perpetual boys—the beachcombers, the divers for pennies, the lion tamers, the test pilots, the climbers of mountains, the negro piano-players. He was of that company, yet greater than they could be, for his eternal boyhood is independent of hearsay memory; it is recorded permanently, I believe, in print.

(ii)

One of our literary parlour games is fond of putting the question: 'How would —— have developed, had he lived longer?' It has been asked about every writer of great talent who has died young—Marlowe, Keats, Rupert Brooke, Sidney Keyes, Alun Lewis, Wilfred Owen, Chatterton. And now it is being asked about Dylan Thomas. I have heard it said that his true future would have become that of a novelist, and again, that of a playwright; the argument being that a creative writer needs a broader canvas to work on as the lyric impulse slackens off with age. *The Doctor and the Devils* is quoted in support of the one theory; *Under Milk Wood* in support of the other. Yet it is my opinion that he would have filled neither rôle—of novelist or playwright—short of a very great and almost incredible change in his nature.

Dylan Thomas lacked the one essential quality of the novelist—the ability (is it patience, persistence, just sheer donkeywork?) to organise experience over a long distance. The novelist is a Miler; Dylan a Hundred Yards Sprinter. His undoubted genius was one of short bursts. Even his stories move at a breathless pace, each bearing its own quietus in its last sentence. They are the tales of a lyric poet. I cannot visualise him as a novelist (any more than one could see

O. Henry) writing serenely on over a course of 90,000 words. It is perhaps the distinction between a broad, and sometimes dull, panoramic view and a series of isolated but excitingly brilliant snapshots. I do not think that it is a question of training but of identity. Stated in its simplest and crudest form, the final problem of the novelist is the problem of a man who must keep at it, must be broken-in and reconciled to sitting at a desk for hour after hour, week after week, month after month. A novel is not to be achieved at a flash, or even a series of flashes, like some kinds of poem and some kinds of story. A writer's typical form depends on his intellectual and emotional *span*. Different writers work in different units of attention. One might justifiably guess that at present Walter de la Mare's fine talent operates best over the span of three short verses; while that of Christopher Fry needs a span of three longish Acts.

However, we must avoid the error of comparing length with quality. Provided each is good of its kind, the surgeon's scalpel is as important as an aircraft carrier. If this were not so we should have to set MacNeice above Andrew Young, MacDiarmid above Robert Graves; and a good short story by Dylan Thomas as of greater value than a long novel by, say, Marie Corelli or Ouida.

The argument against Dylan Thomas as potential playwright is of a similar order. Though he was a splendid actor personally, and shows a strong sense of 'theatre' in *Portrait of the Artist as a Young Dog,* and in his tale of Saturday night adolescence, *The Followers,* his narrative elements were capsules of sensitivity, linked tenuously, where in the theatre they would need to be hard and obvious and strongly vertebrate.

Dylan Thomas gives us a clue himself, in the 'Answers to an Enquiry' which he wrote in *New Verse* twenty years ago. In answer to the question: 'Do you think there can now be a use for narrative poetry?' He said, 'Yes. Narrative is essential. Much of the flat, abstract poetry of the present has no narrative movement, no movement at all, and is consequently dead. There must be *a progressive line, or theme, of movement* in each poem. *The more subjective a poem, the clearer the narrative line*'. (My italics). When we consider the normal connotation of the word 'narrative' and measure it against Dylan Thomas's poems, we see immediately that he meant something else—a mood, a *leit motif*, a series of images; but not a story, a continuous structure of event or characterisation. The theatre is a cruder mechanism than the poem.

Under Milk Wood can give no possible support to any belief that Dylan Thomas might have become a playwright. It is a series of labyrinthine, microscopic insights, magnificently moving in its separate units, but blurred and static when seen as a whole. Nothing seems to *happen* (which makes it so true a picture of a small town, of course) apart from the varied beating of the hearts in the hundred rooms. It bears no more relation to a play than does a clockmaker's shop, where the many machines tick out their day at speeds and tones dictated by their individual mechanisms. Or, to use another metaphor, *Under Milk Wood* is an anthill, which is quite static from a distance of ten yards and only comes to life when observed from ten inches. It is a pointilliste technique too refined for the theatre.

There was nothing new in this; he had always done it. Such early stories as the *Burning Baby, The Orchards* and the one about the witches are full of it. And it is implicit in such later poems as *Fern Hill* or *Poem in October*. He said it all to me in an early letter (which has since been quoted over half the world, from Oxford to Seattle):

'A poem by myself *needs* a host of images because its

centre is a host of images. I make one image—though "make" is not the word; I let, perhaps, an image be made emotionally in me and then apply to it what intellectual and critical forces I possess—let it breed another, let that image contradict the first, make, of the third image bred out of the other two together, a fourth contradictory image, and let them all, within my imposed formal limits, conflict. Each image holds within it the seed of its own destruction, and my dialectal method, as I understand it, is a constant building up and breaking down of the images that come out of the central seed, which is itself destructive and constructive at the same time'.

What he is saying in common terms is that his is a poetry of images, related or unrelated, as they occur to him. It was a method of working ingrained in him, temperamentally, from beginning to end. It is observable in *18 Poems* as in *The Doctor and the Devils*. There was only the slightest concession to clarification as time went on. But of course, as is obvious from such a method, it swamped the narrative, story element. There was visible no movement forwards, no philosophic resolution. The end is in the beginning; and the beginning is a warring cluster of images, whether we call them 'death's feather' and 'wax'—or give them the names of the clamouring personae of *Under Milk Wood*.

(iii)

What of the future? What position in the calendar of poets is Dylan Thomas likely to hold? No-one but a fool would even make a guess, for reputations rise and fall as rhythmically as the waves of the sea. Look at Donne, Hopkins, Clare, Traherne, Stephen Phillips, Owen; almost anybody.

But I feel fairly safe in saying this; that at some future date, and then perhaps only for a short time—but strongly while it lasts—the involuted, the obscure in Dylan Thomas's work will be put aside, perhaps ignored as a foible, and what is left will be reassessed with delight. And it will be found to consist of that most delightful of things—the story of childhood. Dylan Thomas was, despite his Freudian façade, the everlasting boy. He remembered what it all felt like, the sudden joys, the deep humiliations, the balls of dirt between the toes. And no other writer has set it down so movingly, for he completely lacked that tooth-sucking vice of whimsy which devitalises so many records of childhood.

(iv)

But right at the bitter heart of the matter simmers a wry, disturbing suspicion—that Dylan Thomas, in dedicating himself to his own vision, his uninhibited Wonderland of life, brought death a little nearer.

We hear much to-day of ritual sacrifice. Robert Graves and Hugh Ross Williamson make it a credible hypothesis. Now we think we understand the arrow that took off Rufus; and the sad ends of Edward II or of Richard II are made more reasonable.

Dylan Thomas was a dedicated poet, in the sense that he was *called, spoken to from elsewhere, made to utter*. His were the struggles of a Dedicated One who knew, but could not get away. His behaviour in the 'average' life of towns and cities was explicable in such a sense. Among the Aztecs the dedicated one was permitted all he wished, before the pyramid, the obsidian knife.

There is this difference, that the assembled folk about the great stones were relieved to see their sacrifice accepted, for his passing brought prosperity. The death of Dylan Thomas has brought a great sadness. It is some measure of the love and esteem which were generally felt for him that writers of most persuasions have joined in paying tribute to his genius and personality—even those writers at whom he—the Young Rip—cocked a cheekily contemptuous snook. Which is all as it should be in a world too small in genius that it can bear the passing of one of its parts without tears.

(v)

'I, in my intricate image, stride on two levels', he said, not making it too clear what those levels were.

He had the critics confused too, for, whether or not they approved of his work, its force demanded their consideration: and whereas one eminent poet claimed Thomas to have produced 'the most absolute poetry that has been written in our time', another felt sure that his verse was nothing short of 'an unconducted tour of Bedlam'.

And while Edith Sitwell declared that 'a new poet has arisen who shows every promise of greatness', Mr. Louis MacNeice stated his belief, 'He is like a drunk man speaking wildly but rhythmically, pouring out a series of nonsense images, the cumulative effect of which is usually vital and sometimes even seems to have a message—this message being adolescence' *(Modern Poetry, 1938).*

Although Dylan's early poems might have been expressed by a formula (where H = Hopkins, S = Swinburne, J = Joyce, etc.), each element of which was previously well-known to the poetry-reading public, their initial surprise, their impact, was such that they gave the impression of being entirely new, like nothing that had ever before appeared in English letters.

His readers either, like Louis MacNeice, deprecated him or, like Edith Sitwell, expected very great things of him.

And everywhere his admirers sat round the fire watching and waiting for the kettle to boil: a phenomenon which most of them missed, since it had already boiled before they sat down. And the steam came off like this:

> *Light breaks where no sun shines;*
> *Where no sea runs, the waters of the heart*
> *Push in their tides;*
> *And, broken ghosts with glowworms in their heads,*
> *The things of light*
> *File through the flesh where no flesh decks the bones.*
>
> *18 Poems*

That was the essential Thomas, the peak beyond which there is no passing in the same *genre*. With such work, he already ceased to be a 'promising' poet, and became a poet with quite a past.

What does this strange and difficult poetry mean? demanded someone—and Dylan Thomas answered:

'I ask only that my poetry should be taken literally'.

And this would have been a fair enough reply, had the poet adhered to that viewpoint; but Thomas attempted to push on beyond the limits of his stated desire, so that the result became an intricate verbalism and a parody of his earlier work, as in the passage which so often served the late James Agate in his attacks on contemporary poetry:

> *Because the pleasure-bird whistles after the hot wires,*
> *Shall the blind horse sing sweeter?*
> *Convenient bird and beast lie lodged to suffer*
> *The supper and knives of a mood.*
>
> *The Map of Love*

Though I do not imply here that the poem concerned is what Julian Symons might call a 'fake poem'; it seems rather to be

B

an example of what can happen to the poet whose verbal energy is unrefined. It is unlikely that an artist in the throes of creation, or of recording his vision, can see immediately what he has produced. It may contain certain impure elements, or whole passages of inferior worth, which may not become apparent until later reading and emendation. It is even possible that a complete poem might suffer, unwittingly to the poet, from this impurity or inferiority. Yet such a poem might have evolved from a perfectly authentic 'germ', or initial stimulus, which, if it had occurred a day earlier, or a day later, when the balance of the poet's energy and craftsmanship, his mood and awareness, had been different, might have produced a different, possibly more genuine, work of art.

Had all Thomas's poems been of this order, there is little doubt that even his most ardent admirers would have given up the struggle of deciphering his lyrical acrostics. However, his moods of literary mischievousness alternated with phases of a poetic grandeur, as in *The hand that signed the paper,* so that one became temporarily reassured, and hopefully awaited for further manifestations of this magnificent clarity.

It is the story, necessarily confused and confusing, of the poet's journey into the unequivocal light that occupies this book. It is my implicit thesis that he moved little further than the farm-house in the dingle, where the hayfields stood as high as the house: but to get there he had to shake off the nightmare obsession of the imprisoning womb, to become a father himself and so know victory over birth's terrors. Then, moving away from passion—perhaps a little wistfully—he could turn once more to a world outside himself and draw pictures (sometimes caricatures) of creatures other than his immediate self, including the little boy, 'famous among the barns', who was so innocently different from the other Dylan who wrote about him.

Then he had achieved the full circle, and there is perhaps nothing more for a dedicated artist to do.

CHAPTER ONE

Relations to Surrealism

SINCE he has so often in reviews been termed a Surrealist, it seems reasonable to establish as early as possible not only the similarities of ideal between Dylan Thomas and the Surrealists, but also the critical dissimilarities which differentiate his performance from theirs.

So, first, what is Surrealism? What does it set out to do? This is the way its sympathisers defined it:

> SURREALISM, *n*. Pure psychic automatism, by which it is intended to express, verbally, in writing, or by other means, the real process of thought. Thought's dictation, in the absence of all control exercised by the reason and outside all aesthetic or moral preoccupations. It tends definitely to do away with all other psychic mechanisms and to substitute itself for them in *the solution of the principal problems of life.*
>
> ANDRÉ BRETON

> A human being drifts through time like an iceberg, only partly floating above the level of the consciousness. It is the aim of the Surrealist, whether as a painter or as a poet, *to try and realise some of the dimensions and characteristics of his submerged being,* and to do this he resorts to the significant imagery of dreams and dreamlike states of mind.
>
> HERBERT READ from *Art Now*

21

> Surrealism now aims at recreating *a condition which will be in no way inferior to mental derangement*. Its ambition is to lead us to the edge of madness and make us feel what is going on in the magnificently disordered mind of those whom the community shuts up in asylums.

HENRI BARRANGER 'Surrealism in 1931' in *Le Centaure*

The Surrealist Movement began about 1922, having usurped and expelled its older and possibly more amusing rival Dada. 'Negativism, revolt, destruction of all values, Dada was a violent protest against art, literature, morals, society. It spat in the eye of the world. Life is a disgusting riddle, but we can ask harder ones, was the Dadaist attitude. To many intelligent men at this time, suicide seemed to be the one remaining solution to the problem of living, and Dada was a spectacular form of suicide, a manifestation of almost lunatic despair', as David Gascoyne said in *A Short Survey of Surrealism* (Cobden, 1935).

This spectacular form of suicide, with its quaint exhibitions, its reproduction of the Mona Lisa (complete with a handsome pair of moustaches painted on her face, and bearing underneath the inscription: LHOOQ), its poem consisting of the letters of the alphabet, and its enigmatic lavatory bowl, flourished approximately between the years 1916-1922; during which period it did its best to attack all existing values in a grand, delirious revolt.

But the foremost theorists of this period came in the end to realise that the revolutionary anarchy of Dada was in itself yet another tyranny, and they were anxious to avoid restrictions of any kind. 'A new declaration of the rights of man must be made', said the first number of the *Surrealist Revolution,* 1924; and, thereupon, these non-conforming

Dadaists became Surrealists. They believed, 'Dada: negation. Surrealism: negation of negation; a new affirmation,'
and this new affirmation was to take the form of psychic
automatism, in which the imagination should be unshackled
from the tyranny of preconception. In the name of the New
Revolt, all things were to be possible to the believer: 'This
summer the roses are blue; the wood is made of glass',
stated André Breton; 'A corset in July is worth a horde of
rats', and 'He who sows fingernails reaps a torch,' affirmed
Eluard and Péret.

This movement also was to break down accepted values,
to reinstate new systems for the moment, before destroying
them in their turn. Above all, it was to shock the world into
reconsidering its conceptions of reality. . . . 'It is endowed
with that major accent, eternal and modern, which explodes
and leaves a hole in the world of prudently ordained necessities and murmured fairy-stories. . . . For it insolently
militates for a new régime, that of logic related to life not
as a shadow but as a star', said Péret, in *Remove your Hat*.

The grand, carefree days of Dada were over. The lavatory bowl must neglect its ambitions, and return to its
original humdrum existence, and though 'this summer the
roses are blue', the Mona Lisa must forget her translation,
and return to her canvas clean-shaven. For this was the beginning of a New Régime; this was now a Movement with
a Mission.

As David Gascoyne said, 'Surrealism, profiting from the
discoveries of Freud and a few other scientific explorers of
the unconscious, has conceived poetry as being, on the one
hand, a perpetual functioning of the psyche, *a perpetual
flow of irrational thought in the form of images* taking place
in every human mind and needing only a certain predisposi-
tion and discipline in order to be brought to light in the
form of written words (or plastic images), and on the other

hand, a universally valid attitude to experience, *a possible mode of living* (*A Short Survey of Surrealism*).

Now 'Surrealism', like any other catch-phrase, is a label which can easily be attached to any literary or pictorial art that does not comply with accepted formulae, that does not offer its own solution, simply laid out on a salver. So, because of his complexity, his unusually startling and fertile flow of images, and his conceptions of other realities, Dylan Thomas has been connected, in the minds of some readers, with the Surrealists whose ideas and work have gained a publicity in this country simultaneously with the appearance of his poetry. Moreover, statements have been made, and implied, both by the Surrealist and by Dylan Thomas, which would seem to indicate that their respective positions as artists need some elucidation, if only because of their apparent coincidence on many points.

The Surrealists have claimed that their object is 'to try and realise some of the dimensions and characteristics of the submerged being' (the Unconscious), and that in doing so they hope to discover 'a possible mode of living', and 'the solution of the principal problems of life'; while, in *Answers to an Enquiry*, Dylan Thomas has stated his desire to record 'the stripping of the individual darkness, which must, inevitably, cast light upon what has been hidden for too long, and by so doing, make clean the naked exposure. Benefitting by the sight of the light, and the knowledge of the hidden nakedness, poetry must drag further into the clean nakedness of light more even of the hidden causes than Freud could realise'. His poetry is, 'or should be useful to others', he says, 'for its individual recording of that same struggle with which they are necessarily acquainted'.

What both sides are saying is, in effect: We must explore the substance and the limits of the subconscious mind, and, assisted by the resulting knowledge of ourselves, reorganise our attitudes, our reactions to experience, and our modes of living.

Profiting from the discoveries of Freud, they are not content with a mere visual reproduction in words of what they see in the outer world; they are not Nature poets, or Descriptive poets, or Political poets. Although they have both expressed sympathies with Communism, there is no direct, objective sermonising in their poetry. If they are religious or narrative poets ever—and Dylan Thomas states that he is very sympathetic towards narrative poetry—the narrative and the religion will be subjective, and arising from the individual subconscious.

So far, it appears, the Surrealist poets and Dylan Thomas receive both impulse and material from a similar source; and, basically, their conceptions of the art they practise are of a like nature. Whereas the Surrealists believe that poetry is 'a perpetual flow of irrational thought *in the form of images*', Dylan Thomas has said, '*A poem by myself needs a host of images*. I make one image, though "make" is not the word: I let, perhaps, an image be made emotionally in me and then apply to it what intellectual and critical forces I possess; let it breed another; let that image contradict the first, make, of the third image, bred out of the other two together, a fourth contradictory image, and let them all, within my imposed formal limits, conflict'.

Fundamentally, it seems, the *image* is the important factor in the poetry of both conceptions:

And now the horns of England, in the sound of shape,
Summon your snowy horsemen, and the four-stringed hill,
Over the sea-gut loudening, sets a rock alive;
Hurdles and guns and railings, as the boulders heave,
Crack like a spring in a vice, bore breaking April,
Spill the lank folly's hunter and the hard-held hope.

25 Poems

DYLAN THOMAS

The Very Image

To René Magritte

An image of my grandmother
her head appearing upside-down upon a cloud
the cloud transfixed on the steeple
of a deserted railway-station
far away.

An image of an aqueduct
With a dead crow hanging from the first arch
a modern style chair from the second
a fir-tree lodged in the third
and the whole scene sprinkled with snow.

An image of the piano tuner
with a basket of prawns on his shoulder
and a fire-screen under his arm
his moustache made of clay-clotted twigs
and his cheeks daubed with wine.

. . . . And all these images
and many others
are arranged like waxworks
in model bird cages
about six inches high.

DAVID GASCOYNE

Images there are, in profusion, in the work of each of these poets: but when that has been said the apparent similarity ends, for the Surrealists, by their repudiation of the conscious mind, deny the importance and prohibit the practice of poetic craftsmanship, and, with pure psychic automatism as a substitute, discard all form as being an effete cult of the conventional *bourgeoisie*.

The images of Dylan Thomas, on the other hand, may

come as spontaneously as those of Breton or Péret or Gascoyne, but while these poets, because of their artistic beliefs, make no attempt to select, or to write critically, he, as he tells us himself, applies to his images what intellectual and critical forces he possesses, allowing them to exist only within certain formal limits.

The distinction lies, then, between the controlled and the uncontrolled subconscious; and here arises a problem which all serious Surrealists must have to face:

Is all material which presents itself to the writer by psychic automatism of an equal artistic value?

It would seem that such material from the subconscious must of necessity be unequal in quality, and must need the control of a selective mind. It is this discipline of his raw material, this obedience to the dictates of his self-imposed form, which makes Dylan Thomas a superior craftsman to, and a better poet than, most of the Surrealists.

Complete absence of conscious control must, inevitably, result in an artistic anarchy, against which all criticism will be powerless, and for which no development will be possible.

Apart from this question of craftsmanship, it will be accepted by all critics to whom art means anything more dignified than the creation of mud-pies and wire-puzzles, that poetry must be 'memorable speech'. Yet Surrealism denies us this, giving us by way of substitute succession after succession of bewildering images, which succeed only in bludgeoning the mind into insensibility. And when we do chance to remember anything at all, it is likely to be such lines and images as:

The strident crying of red eggs,

or

The quarrel between the boiled chicken and the ventriloquist,
had for us the meaning of a cloud of dust;

which makes a poor showing when set beside those phrases of Dylan Thomas, which come so readily and so forcibly to the mind:

Some let me make you of the vowelled beeches,
Some of the oaken voices, from the roots,
Of many a thorny shire tell you notes,
Some let me make you of the water's speeches.

18 Poems

Light and dark are not enemies
But one companion.

25 Poems

It is very difficult to understand how this Movement, concerned only with the writing down of images, so that each image rapidly supersedes its predecessor and is immediately superseded itself, can make statements of any philosophic or critical value at all; and it is impossible to see how these images, startling and colourful though they may be for the moment, can help in the resolution of any conflict known to that great body of humanity which the Surrealists profess to support.

André Breton has assured us that Surrealism has within itself the power to solve the principal problems of life; and David Gascoyne states that the movement is 'a universally valid attitude to experience, a possible mode of living'.

One can agree with Breton and Gascoyne here only if they mean that by treating life as a great joke one can, if one is sufficiently reckless or unambitious, get away with most things.

This, however, is a selfish attitude and is ultimately invalid: whereas the vagaries of any one person might be tolerated by his fellows, the universal application of Surrealism would result in a chaotic discomfort and breakdown of life. How inconvenient it would be, should the driver of the 5.30 train decide he would not start his engine until 8.45. How catastrophic it would be if all surgeons agreed to operate only with meat-axes.

It seems that Dylan Thomas was more sincere, constructive and believable in his search for other realities, and other possible modes of living when he said:

> *Which is the world? Of our two sleepings, which*
> *Shall fall awake when cures and their itch*
> *Raise up this red-eyed earth?*

It is the question that Calderón asks in 'La Vida es Sueño'. If Dylan Thomas had found the answer to it, the result would have been helpful. But the Surrealists, charmed by the strident crying of their red eggs, finding one 'reality' as good as another, and the next as good as that one, have seemed to turn round and round, like dogs settling down for the night, until their weakest members die of sheer boredom, and the strongest stop to see the world going on without them.

CHAPTER TWO

General Characteristics

Poetry is the rhythmic movement from an over-clothed blindness to a naked vision. My poetry is the record of my individual struggle from darkness towards some measure of light. My poetry is, or should be, useful to others for its individual recording of that same struggle with which they are necessarily acquainted. . . . Poetry, recording the stripping of the individual darkness, must, inevitably, cast light upon what has been hidden for too long, and, by so doing, make clean the naked exposure. . . . It must drag further into the clean nakedness of light more even of the hidden causes than Freud could realise. *New Verse* October 1934

T H E S E words, written in answer to an Enquiry made by Geoffrey Grigson, are possibly one of the keys to the poetry of Dylan Thomas. They constitute a manifesto.

The poet's admitted desire, then, was to expose all his experiences, remembered and forgotten, to drag the depths of the mind, and, by displaying what he found there, to himself and to his audience, to provide himself and them, should their experience coincide with his, with a means of readjustment to living, which, with that self-knowledge, that reintegration with other personalities, should logically result from a sound psychological readjustment, mental health and a fuller and more valid mode of living. Nothing of which is as new or as startling as we might have expected, since it is presumably the basic impulse of everyone who writes after adolescence, to 'get things straight', conventionally stated, by giving them an entity outside himself. What is very probably new and startling in the work of Dylan Thomas is that, in dragging into light his versions of 'the hidden causes' which he mentions, he has given an articulate voice to other parts of the body than the romantic heart—to the glands and the nerves, that is—and has, in considerable measure, freed them from the poetically sterile reason.

Unlike so many of his contemporaries, Thomas did not turn either critically or admiringly towards experimental political systems over the seas.

In October 1934, answering the *New Verse* Enquiry, he did state: 'I take my stand with any revolutionary body that asserts it to be the right of all men to share, equally and impartially, every production of man from man and from the sources of production at man's disposal, for only through such an essentially revolutionary body can there be the possibility of a communal art'.

By 1938, when I was discussing this statement with him, Thomas felt that he should withdraw it, and that it no longer applied. This repudiation of an adolescent belief was completely justified. Thomas could hope for little support from a People's Government, unless the whole nature of his art suffered a change. His obscurity and preoccupation with the Self would be the last thing a Totalitarian State would support.

Nor is it conceivable that a communal art could flourish, based on Thomas's very individual and often uncommunicable preoccupations.

Although he was suitably interested in most phases of life, his impulse came primarily from within his own body. He is the poet within the poet, and is generally dependent upon no externalities for his subject. This is one of his main contributions to poetry: he has given voices and eyes to that part of the being which had formerly been dumb and blind; he has given the body a poetic aura, which might almost be called another, less conventionally rational, mind; and he has shown how this 'mind' might think, or, at least, the shape its statements might take, rhythmically expressed.

Stylistically Thomas is more often than not formal. His stanza-patterns, though individual, are usually uniform, and his use of balanced alliteration and half-rhyme is unoriginal. His technical innovation lies rather in his vocabulary, in his imagery, which affect the reader primarily and principally through the emotions; an effect which they do not seem to create as much as emphasise.

And since Thomas appeals only infrequently to the intellect his poems stand or fall by their coincidence at the time of reading with a similar mood or emotion on the part of the reader. But when this coincidence occurs, the result is intoxicating:

> *Especially when the October wind*
> *With frosty fingers punishes my hair,*
> *Caught by the crabbing sun I walk on fire*
> *And cast a shadow crab upon the land,*
> *By the sea's side hearing the noise of birds,*
> *Hearing the raven cough in winter sticks,*
> *My busy heart who shudders as she talks*
> *Sheds the syllabic blood and drains her words.*

18 Poems

Such exciting rhetoric and imagery grow out of a rich and profuse, even if inaccurate, word-sense.

Conversely, few poets in recent times have shown us such tenseness in their imagery as we may find here: 'The thickets antlered like deer'; or 'The wagging clock', 'The syllabic blood', 'The loud hill of Wales', 'The star-gestured children', all chosen from one poem; or such a splendid illusion of Shakespearian rhetoric as:

> *And death shall have no dominion.*
> *No more may gulls cry at their ears*
> *Or waves break loud on the seashores;*
> *Where blew a flower may a flower no more*
> *Lift its head to the blows of the rain;*
>
> *25 Poems*

At times, through all this excitement of words, is heard the faint but unmistakable echo of other days and other styles:

> *And death shall have no dominion,*
> *Dead men naked they shall be one*
> *With the man in the wind and the west moon.*
>
> *25 Poems*

> *In Spring we cross our foreheads with the holly,*
> *Heigh ho the blood and the berry,*
> *And nail the merry squires to the trees.*
>
> *18 Poems*

> *In the beginning was the three-pointed star,*
> *One smile of light across the empty face.*
>
> *18 Poems*

Or, as in the following passage, there is sometimes a more direct allusion:

> *'Time shall not murder you', he said,*
> *'Nor the green nought be hurt . . .'*
>
> *25 Poems*

C

so strangely reminiscent of:

> *Age cannot wither her, nor custom stale*
> *Her infinite variety . . .*

All these echoes give an overtone to the poet's statements and produce the illusion that he is working on a number of planes simultaneously, or that his work has a polyphony of matter and manner in some degree comparable to that of a fugal composition in music; they are part of his stock-in-trade as a musical, as opposed to an intellectual poet.

It is in the use of overtones, and in the evocation of emotional 'atmosphere' that Dylan Thomas is most frequently successful:

> *Light breaks on secret lots,*
> *On tips of thought where thoughts smell in the rain.*
>
> > 18 Poems

> *I see the summer children in their mothers,*
> *Divide the night and day with fairy thumbs;*
>
> > 18 Poems

Here is what earlier critics might have called 'the faery alchemy': and, looking at the poet's work in retrospect, this is not his least considerable contribution to the literature of our time.

So much for Thomas's obvious assets: on the debit side, he has been variously accused. Some, while condoning the vagaries of Hopkins, have deprecated his obscurity. Others have cavilled at his 'slipshod use of words', at the monotony of some of his rhythmic patterns, and at the limitations of his theme.

Thomas's rhythmic monotony was the result of his early fixation on the iambic pentameter, the most suitable metre for the young writer who wished to make a grand and dramatic gesture. One of his technical battles throughout the whole of his poetic development, was the discovery of a substitute for the pentameter. This battle was never won: from time to time Thomas slipped back into his earlier metrical habits; though it must be stated that his latest work (especially such poems as *Poem in October, 1945,* and *Vision and Prayer*) showed the poet's achievement of a considerable rhythmic freedom.

In answer to the first objection, however, one must admit that Dylan Thomas is obscure, and must remain obscure to all whose emotional experiences are dissimilar from his, though principally so to those who will make no effort to recognise the voices of the body, and to those who demand, from everything they may encounter in life and Art, a mathematical equation, or a prose equivalent.

Whereas, for ordinary and utilitarian purposes, a series of words must express thought, the simplest form which this thought can take being that judgment of which the common verbal form is a proposition, $A = B$; for artistic purposes, which require a peculiar use of language, 'meaning' should be dependent on recognition of Pattern, and on any excitement, emotional or intellectual, of colour, sound or shape, which carries with it a satisfaction or an inner fusion.

And, while agreeing that the poet's frequent metaphysical enquiry is sometimes alarming, it seems appropriate to state that in his short stories, and in a number of those verses contained in his later works, Dylan Thomas showed that his development would be towards an increased clarity, in the generally accepted sense.

The other objections are, in the main, scarcely worth arguing about: the poet is primarily concerned with Man, through birth, copulation, to death, as has been frequently stated. Life is a limited process, after all, and only human conceit could make it other than it is; so, if the successions of glandular and other physical images seem tiring and unreal, then the sooner all dissatisfied critics abandon the poetry of Thomas, the better: for it seems unlikely that his talent would ever throw off completely the qualities which they deplore.

The words of the poet himself seem adequate at first sight in reply to the charge of slipshod writing, until one has had the opportunity, not only of reading a considerable part of Thomas's work, but also of standing twenty years away from its first appearance. Then it is apparent that the poet's theory of creating an image, of letting that image war with another image to produce a third image, and so on, is little more (or less) than a rationalisation of a process which may only be guessed at by the creator of the poem. In actual fact, Thomas's poems seem to proceed by a simple associative mechanism, controlled by his rhythmic scheme and fed by his cultural and verbal habits. Again and again this mechanism takes the same turn, though in different circumstances, leading one to suppose that the poet had a certain almost inflexible stock of verbal habits or responses, which occurred unceasingly and with only the slightest variation as he grew older, to whatever initial stimuli his original poetic impulse produced. The tricks of the Slightly Older Dog are the same as those of the Young Dog—but made public with the knowledge, perhaps uncertain previously, of the reading public's reactions to such tricks; and in this way, bad habits are perpetuated, together with good ones: and the only criterion comes from the readers' and not the writer's development as the years pass.

It seems that a more serious fault of Dylan Thomas's early poems is their *diffuseness*. They have not that concentric movement round a central image which gives a unity to the work of many poets, so that one gets the impression that each of his poems might constitute a section from a longer poem.[1]

Here, once again, it appears that the poet recognised his fault, for, in *Deaths and Entrances,* with few exceptions, each piece of work stands independent of the others, as a

[1] These are the comments of Dylan Thomas upon my criticism of his diffuseness:

'When you say that I have not Cameron's or Madge's "concentric movement round a central image", you are not accounting for the fact that it consciously is not my method to move concentrically round a central image. A poem by Cameron needs no more than one image; it moves around one idea, from one logical point to another, making a full circle. A poem by myself *needs* a host of images, because its centre is a host of images. I make one image—though "make" is not the word; I let, perhaps, an image be "made" emotionally in me and then apply to it what intellectual and critical forces I possess—let it breed another, let that image contradict the first, make, of the third image bred out of the other two together, a fourth contradictory image, and let them all, within my imposed formal limits, conflict. Each image holds within it the seed of its own destruction, and my dialectal method, as I understand it, is a constant building up and breaking down of the images that come out of the central seed, which is itself destructive and constructive at the same time.

'What I want to try to explain—and it's necessarily vague to me— is that the *life* in any poem of mine cannot move concentrically round a central image; the life must come out of the centre; an image must be born and die in another; and any sequence of my images must be a sequence of creations, recreations, destructions, contradictions. I cannot, either—as Cameron does, and as others do, and this primarily explains his and their writing round the central image—make a poem out of a single motivating experience; I believe in the simple thread of action through a poem, but that is an intellectual thing aimed at lucidity through narrative. My object is, as you say, conventionally "to get things straight". Out of the inevitable conflict of images—inevitable, because of the creative, recreative, destructive and contradictory nature of the motivating centre, the womb of war—I try to make that momentary peace which is a poem. I do not want a poem of mine to be, nor can it be, a circular piece of experience placed neatly outside the living stream of time from which it came; a poem of mine is, or should be, a water-tight section of the stream that is flowing all ways, all warring images within it should be reconciled for that small stop of time. I agree that each of my earlier poems might appear to constitute a section from one long poem; that is because I was not successful in making a momentary peace with my images at the correct moment; images were left dangling over the formal limits, and dragged the poem into another; the warring stream ran on over the insecure barriers, the fullstop armistice was pulled and twisted raggedly on into a conflicting series of dots and dashes'.

unity in itself; though it would be foolish to imagine that recognition by the poet of a 'fault' should be the first step to an elimination of that 'fault'. Thomas went his own way: he blew as fecklessly as any spring gale, sometimes seeming to come from the right direction and with purpose, but often spasmodically and unrepentantly directionless. That is how it is; and, in a cultural tradition such as ours, of indefinite laxity, how it should be.

CHAPTER THREE

Some Influences

IT IS ONE of the functions of the serious poet, owed both to himself and to posterity, that under his hands the language he uses should be transmuted by his own force and personality into something finer for his purpose, and more adequate for the expression of what future generations with their expanded horizons, need to say. Dylan Thomas, following in that line of modern innovators which starts perhaps with Hopkins and develops through Pound, Eliot and Auden, in such an alchemist of words. An individual of some emotional strength and sensitivity, he has shaped language to his feelings, and has left English poetry in a different state from that in which he found it; and, what is more, he has stamped his own personality upon it in such a way as to leave little doubts concerning his literary talent.

It is true that such writers as Doughty and, in more recent days, James Joyce have exercised the language to their hand; but in both of these cases, this exercise has been a purely individual one, mirroring their own very singular and untransmittable personalities, and without attraction for others to use it for the externalisation of other problems. Doughty and Joyce have transmuted language, for their own ends, which are not the ends of others. They stand, therefore, at the blind ends of literary *culs-de-sac*. Thomas, on the other hand, has had the good fortune to possess a talent which has enabled his younger contemporaries to effect more easily a solution of their personal literary problems. It is doubtful, for instance, whether many young poets could have written their poems so early had not Thomas prepared the way for them. Though, since Thomas's necessities are not theirs, it is not entirely a good thing for their talents that these poets should persist in their derivation. Such an innovator as Thomas should serve at the most, as a literary focal point, to be discarded as soon as a young poet's field of vision changes.

This is not to say that Thomas himself has never worked under the influence of other poets. It is hard to see how a young writer, sensible to life and literature, and for whom that literature is an organic part of life, could, as a receptive instrument, ignore what has happened and what is happening around him as he writes. But the talent of a writer depends upon his ability to assimilate such influences, so that they form bases rather than superstructure of his work. His duty to himself, and to the poets from whom he has derived, is to give these borrowings fresh life and personality, to absorb them into his own living, and only to allow them a sight of the outside world again when they have become his own personal weapons, with which he may tackle his own individual problems. Conversely, it is probably the case that those readers who derive little satisfaction from any particular poet are living under different compulsions from that poet. Their problems are not his, and in consequence, they may not fully realise what he is about. Then again, it is likely that every reader 'writes' the poem he wishes to read; or, in other words, sees in a poem what he wants to see, not necessarily that which the poet most wanted to write. Such poets as the Augustans, Roy Campbell, or Wordsworth, may allow no such perceptual elasticity: but Hart Crane, Swinburne, Hopkins, Thomas and even T. S. Eliot will leave many opportunities to their readers of personal interpretation.

Apart from the general influence which the ballads, fairy-stories and the Scriptures have had on Thomas, there are perhaps five individual poets whose methods have been absorbed into the work of Dylan Thomas. In order of the apparent strength of their influence they are Gerard Manley Hopkins, Hart Crane, Swinburne, Rimbaud and Francis Thompson, and it must be remembered that one is considering here the influence on Thomas of poets only: if one were to add prose-writers to the list, then James Joyce and Henry Miller would have to be discussed. The first is a technical influence, operating so strongly at times that it is possible to read Thomas (especially the 'Sonnets' from a *Work in Progress*) indistinguishably from a page of Joyce. Miller's influence *(Aller-Retour New York, Tropic of Cancer* and *Tropic of Capricorn)* is one of attitude: it is the attitude of a highly sensitive man who can look in all directions at once, recording what he sees and feels without distinction of topic.

It has been fashionable during the last generation to cite Hopkins as a dominant influence whenever the work of a new poet has been under discussion; often with little justification and no profit to reader, writer or critic. But the case of Dylan Thomas is one where the derivation from the earlier poet is so organic and pronounced as to deserve close attention; and, since such an examination is impossible in a short introduction, I have given up a whole chapter to the topic later on in this book.

The influence of Hart Crane, unlike that of Hopkins, is more difficult to estimate, since it may be the case that a likeness of perception and reaction in both poets has resulted in the almost independent use of similar technical approaches with which to solve almost identical problems.

At any rate, if there is a direct influence it is limited, and seldom operates outside the bounds of vocabulary and phraseology. But within these limits, the similarities are at least striking:

> *Twin shadowed halves: the breaking second holds*
> *In each the skin alone, and so it is*
> *I crust a plate of vibrant mercury*
> *Borne cleft to you, and brother in the half . . .*
>
> *Let the same nameless gulf beleaguer us—*
> *Alike suspend us from atrocious sums*
> *Built floor by floor on shafts of steel that grant*
> *The plummet heart, like Absalom, no streams.*
>
> HART CRANE Recitative
>
> *Anchises' navel, dripping of the sea,—*
> *The lands Erasmus dipped in gleaming tides,*
> *Gathered the voltage of blown blood and vine;*
> *Delve upward for the new and scattered wine,*
> *O brother-thief of time, that we recall.*
>
> HART CRANE *For the Marriage of Faustus and Helen*

These lines look very much like the work of Dylan Thomas, even at first reading, and inspection will show that much of the similarity lies in Hart Crane's occasional phrases: 'Twin shadowed halves', 'the breaking second', 'brother in the half', 'the plummet heart', 'Absalom', 'blown blood and vine', might all be the words of Thomas, and so might the significant physical references and sea-imagery. But here the likeness ends: nor is it possible to observe in any other parts of the two poems by Hart Crane, from which these extracts were taken, any other lines or words which might have come naturally from the pen of Dylan Thomas. Because of this, and not because of the poet's own comments, it seems that Hart Crane's influence to be fairly limited, and possibly fortuitous. When I mentioned it to him once, Thomas replied, 'Three or four years ago, a poet who had read some of my work told me that the most obvious modern influence in my poetry was Crane. And he was astonished, and at first unbelieving, when I told him that I had never heard of Crane before. He showed me some of Crane's poems then, and I could certainly see what he meant: there were, indeed, two or three almost identical bits of phrasing, and much of the actual sound seemed similar. Since then I've read all Crane's poems, and though I now see the resemblance between his poetry and mine to be very slight, I can understand that some people might still think I had come under his influence'.

It is probable that Thomas, as a schoolboy poet almost, came upon a small section of Hart Crane's work, *Recitative* and *Faustus and Helen* for instance, and in such work discovered a focal point for his own writing. It would, for example, be possible to evolve a comprehensive literary style, with developments and decorations to meet new situations, from a *single element* of another poet's style. That is, supposing the poet who provides this focal point is himself a sensitive, vital and complex mechanism.

Swinburne's influence is even less certain, resulting perhaps merely in rhythmic experiments and verbal play, and not in ideology or vocabulary. And, since no definitely derivative stylisms may be quoted, it is only possible here to offer certain examples from the work of Dylan Thomas which seem to show that Swinburnian love of music, that emotional, repetitive and alliterative rush of words, which Michael Roberts has called the 'intoxicated singsong' of Swinburne:

> *And all and all the dry worlds couple,*
> *Ghost with her ghost contagious man . . .*

Flower, flower the people's fusion,
O light in zenith, the coupled bud,
And flame in the flesh's vision.

18 Poems

When their bones are picked clean and the clean bones gone.

25 Poems

Nevertheless, in spite of his love for sounds, 'Musique avant toute chose' is not the overriding desire of Dylan Thomas. What matters more to him is the metaphysical search, to which the music is incidental. Though it must be acknowledged that, while the poet may, in the first verse or even the first line of a poem, begin his work by stating his thesis, or by externalising a controlled poetic impulse which has come to him, the later stages of his poem may proceed and succeed each other almost by an associative process, one image dictating the next, either because of an association of meaning, or of music. Thomas's ear for jocular echoes is sensitive, and this at times results in an elevated form of poetic punning which might lead his non-admirers to belittle the rest of his musical talent. The poet has said, moreover, 'My poems do not flow. They are rather hewn . . .' and whenever the work of hewing becomes at all difficult, the music takes second place.

It is perhaps this musical quality of some of Thomas's lines that has suggested to certain critics the comparison with Rimbaud. There is, it is true, in the work of both poets, the metamorphosis of words to that state when 'le langage en nous prend une valeur moins d'expression que de signe; les mots fortuits qui montent à la surface de l'esprit, le refrain, l'obsession d'une phrase continuelle, forment une espèce d'incantation.'[1] Both poets believed in the 'systematic

---

[1] M. Paul Claudel, *Preface* to Rimbaud's works.

derangement of the senses'. Thomas carried this belief to another plane, and subscribes to the systematic derangement of meanings and sequences hitherto fixed.

> . . . . *the man in the wind and the west moon*
>
> *25 Poems*

is an example of this derangement (it can be observed all through his work and has come to be a verbal habit with him), in which the poet mixes the two images: 'The man in the moon' and 'the west wind'. No one, apart from the contemporary Surrealists, has used this device of derangement to such a degree as Rimbaud and Dylan Thomas. The incantation, perhaps a little more controlled in Thomas, they hold in common, just as they do the colourful and exotic image:

> *Glaciers, soleils d'argent, flots nacreux, cieux de braises*
> *Echouages hideux au fond des golfes bruns*
> *Où les serpents géants dévorés des punaises*
> *Choient des arbres tordus avec de noirs parfums.*
>
> RIMBAUD *Bateau Ivre*

> *(Icebergs and silver suns, pearl waves and brazier skies*
> *And where in deep brown gulfs the stranded horrors lurk,*
> *Where the gigantic serpents, preyed upon by lice,*
> *Crash down from twisted trees, amid black-smelling mirk!)*
>
> *Trans.* NORMAN CAMERON.

Similarly, there is in both poets an intensity, a violence, a frightening perception of death and corruption: and a love of the distorted image, dragged from the dark despair of the adolescent soul. The sea-image occurs so frequently in Thomas that one half-suspects the direct influence of the *Bateau Ivre*; and the Welsh poet's *Ballad of the Long-legged bait* confirms such a suspicion.

It might be, however, that Dylan's Freudian concept of poetry has led him to the image direct, just as his Celtic ancestors were drawn to the sea and the river in their tribal pantheism.

But in spite of these similarities, there is relatively little in the poetry of Dylan Thomas that has definitely come by direct derivation from Rimbaud; little that the Welsh poet might not have written had Rimbaud never put pen to paper. Rimbaud cannot therefore be classed as a predominating influence; he was a young poet who, sensible to the spiritual decay of his France, reacted in an approximately similar manner—allowing for differences in environment and culture—to another young poet, in another country, in another period of dissolution and Pre-war despair.

The influence of Francis Thompson is the most difficult to display on the printed page, though Dylan Thomas acknowledges it. Certainly Thompson employs such paradoxes as:

> *Does the fish soar to find the ocean,*
> *The eagle plunge to find the air. . . . ?*

which are on a similar plane of thought to Dylan's most easily comprehended passages. But in the main, the influence is seen in Dylan's early concept of compound words, allied to an urgent moving towards a spiritual goal; a movement which is made public most clearly in his latest collection, *Deaths and Entrances*.

Finally, though a difficult one, the language of Dylan Thomas is not a 'private' language in the sense that Auden's often is. Thomas is obscure not as the personal allusion to friends is obscure, but as the depths of the spirit are obscure; those fundamental reactions and images, primitive and unsophisticated. So, in this manner only is he a private rather than a social poet. Always his concern was unity within the individual body before unity in the State. As he says, 'Whatever is hidden should be made naked. To be stripped of darkness is to be clean'.

His poetry, then, shows him as the Freudian 'sick man', whose world is only made complete by his own art. Those of his readers who are 'sick' in the same way, will find in Thomas a relief from their malady, a reintegration of the personality in a world created in their own image. For them, Dylan Thomas will be a prophet: and, what is more, a prophet on a level unexplored by those poets whose craftsman-repressions have led them to sift and refine their original poetic impulses to that stage when they can be comprehended by the greatest number of readers.

There have been many poets whose attraction has been that they have put into pictures the cosy, nostalgic, known world of their readers' waking life: but Dylan Thomas will be the meat of the man whose primitive wonder, newly awakened, demands a fresh, if unbalanced world, in which he may declare his own dreams unselfconsciously.

CHAPTER FOUR

The Debt to Hopkins

(i)

We can find in this poet's work the two elements which have been mentioned: (*a*) a passionate emotion which seems to try to utter all its words in one, (*b*) a passionate intellect which is striving at once to recognise and explain both the singleness and division of the accepted Universe. But to these must be added a passionate sense of the details of the world without and the world within, a passionate consciousness of all kinds of experience.

CHARLES WILLIAMS *Introduction* to Hopkin's Poems

O then if in my lagging lines you miss
The roll, the rise, the carol, the creation . . .

G. M. HOPKINS

GERARD MANLEY HOPKINS, Jesuit priest and a contemporary of Swinburne, exercised a profound influence over a large number of contemporary poets, and particularly over the younger ones. In fact, he may be classed as a prime technical influence, for no other poet, not excluding T. S. Eliot, has been responsible for such a show of technical assimilation.

This, on consideration of Hopkin's dates, might seem surprising. Why, if we must go back to the last century for our models, did we not choose one of the 'successful' poets,

Meredith, Rossetti, or Swinburne? Why do we bow to the
ghost of an obscure Jesuit priest, whose work was read by
few in his own lifetime, and fewer in ours until the sponsor-
ship of his poems by the late Laureate.

One answer to these questions is not hard to find, and it
is this: Gerard Manley Hopkins was a poet of conflict, of
intensity and rebellion in a way, and to a degree unap-
proached by any other poet of his period. His work shows
a tension, a dissatisfaction with accepted formulae, yet a
hope for the future, which young poets, nurtured on *The
Waste Land*, and already becoming reactionary to it, could
most easily and most sincerely take as a model. The Depression, once stated, is barren and sterile; later comes a reaction, a renewed hope, and the tremendously vital work of
Hopkins pointed the way to consummation.

Technically, he is the most surprising poet of his generation. His alliterations and inversions were perhaps not
startling (only in so far as he employed them as a means of
elucidating his content: whereas, with his contemporaries,
Meredith, and particularly Swinburne, music was the 'avant
toute chose', so that in their work the matter runs parallel
with the manner and not together with it); but the violence
of his syntax, his 'accumulated masses of nouns, verbs, ad-
jectives and adverbs, unleavened by prepositions or con-
junctions'[1] impress the reader immediately and forcefully
as the work of an outstanding individual mind: 'a passionate
intellect which is striving at once to recognise and explain
both the singleness and division of the accepted Universe'.

> *I am soft sift*
> *In an hourglass—at the wall*
> *Fast, but mined with a motion, a drift,*
> *And it crowds and it combs to the fall;*

[1] Michael Roberts *The Faber Book of Modern Verse*

D

I steady as water in a well, to a poise, to a
    pane,
But roped with, always, all the way down from
    the tall
    Fells of flanks of the voel, a vein
Of the Gospel proffer, a principle, Christ's gift.

The Wreck of the Deutschland

Quite as revolutionary and as startling are Hopkin's advanced metrical schemes, his 'outrides', and the complicated internal harmonies of his rhythmic counterpoint. His changing rhythms and his shifting stresses mirror the man: they are his conflicts, even when reconciled in what is an apparent contentment:

Óur évening is over us, óur night/whélms, whélms, ánd will
    end us.
Only the beakleaved boughs dragonish/damask the tool
    smooth bleak light, black,
Ever so black on it. Óur tale, O óur oracle/Lét life, wáned,
    ah lét life wind
Off hér once skéined, stained, véined variéty/ úpon, all ón
    twó spools; párt, pen, páck.
Now her áll in twó flocks, twó folds—black, white;/right,
    wrong; reckon but, reck but, mind
But thése two; wáre of a wórld where but these/twó tell,
    each off the óther; of a rack
Where, a self-wrung, self-strung, sheathe—and shelterless,/
    thóughts agáinst thoughts ín groans grínd.

Spelt from the Sibyl's Leaves

The metrical signs themselves hint at that complexity which the poet recognised within himself, and show his wish to unravel and to explain.

Important as Hopkins was, however, to the younger poets, it is to his manner rather than his fundamental matter that their derivation mainly belonged. They recognised the conflict in his way of writing, but could not reconcile the conflict in his mind with that in their own. Those poets most frequently indebted to Hopkins employed his stylisms decoratively, and not as a means to elucidation.

Hopkins's search for God and his contentions with God are disregarded as being irrelevant. So Rex Warner, in *Lapwing,* gives us a fine picture of a bird (and maybe something of the poet); but his model *The Windhover; To Christ our Lord,* is more than a visual description: at the least, it is the glory of God in a bird.

Dylan Thomas is one of the few poets to have learned both from the manner and the matter of Gerard Manley Hopkins how to tackle his own independent technical and spiritual problems. But those who look for 'the roll, the rise, the carol, the creation' in the work of this modern poet will be disappointed: it is not there. Where there is a lyricism at all in Thomas, it is in the contemplation of his own processes, and not in the sight of a bird. And, whereas Hopkins might cry aloud in ecstasy for all to hear, in Thomas there is only 'the midnight of a chuckle'.

In other respects there is, however, a deal of resemblance between the two poets. Most particularly there is the similarity in origin of their sources of poetic energy: both look within, to find tension and disorder; both experience that 'important moral conflict, related to an outer . . . intellectual conflict', as Michael Roberts observes later. Their methods of combating this disorder are individual: while Hopkins calls out to God, throwing the light of heaven upon his anguish, Thomas again looks inwards, and as a God unto himself, analyses and diagnoses for his own disorder:

God, lover of souls, swaying considerate scales,
Complete thy creature dear O where it fails,
Being a mighty master, being a father and fond.

In the Valley of the Elwy

So pleads the one, almost sure of the success of his prayers.
Am I not father, too, and the ascending boy,
Am I not all of you?

25 Poems

shouts the modern poet, proud in his self-sufficiency. But
the uncertainty is there, and the inner conflict is never fully
resolved, in God or in the poet's self.

(ii)

Perhaps the most convincing method of emphasising the
similarities between these two poets is that of quoting certain major comments on the one, and observing how closely
and how appropriately the same criticisms might have
been used in reference to the other.

'The very race of the words and the lines hurries on our
emotion; our minds are left behind, not, as in Swinburne,
because they have to suspend their labour until it is wanted,
but because they cannot work at a quick enough rate'.[1]

Nowhere may we find, in so few words, a criticism so
explanatory, if only superficially so, of the work of Dylan
Thomas. The aptness of this comment is obvious in almost
all of his work, and particularly in *18 Poems* and the last
few pages of *25 Poems*.

How now my flesh, my naked fellow,
Dug of the sea, the glanded morrow,
Worm in the scalp, the staked and fallow,
All all and all, the corpse's lover,

[1] Charles Williams, *Introduction to Poems of G. M. Hopkins (O.U.P.)*

Skinny as sin, the foaming marrow,
All of the flesh, the dry world's lever.

18 Poems

And from the windy West came two-gunned Gabriel
From Jesu's sleeve trumped up the king of spots,
The sheath-decked jacks, queen with a shuffled heart;
Said the fake gentleman in suit of spades,
Black-tongued and tipsy from salvation's bottle,
Rose my Byzantine Adam in the night;

25 Poems

There is an energy here, 'a passionate emotion which seems to try to utter all its words in one', which is equalled only by:

Cloud-puff-ball, torn-tufts, tossed pillows/flaunt forth, then
chevy on an air—
built thoroughfare: heaven roysterers, in gay gangs/they
throng: they glitter in marches.
Down roughcast, down dazzling whitewash,/wherever an
elm arches,
Shive lights and shadow tackle in long/lashes lace, lance
and pair.

That Nature is a Heracleitan Fire

The breathless race is the same; the goal is possibly the same, though the gait of the runners is different.

'The single pursuit of even the most subordinate artistic intention gives unity, significance, mass to a poet's work'.[1]

The most vehement critic of the poetry of Dylan Thomas will be unable to deny its force and unity of purpose. There

[1] Middleton Murry, 'Gerard Manley Hopkins' (*Aspects of Literature,* Cape, 1934). Here the critic is explaining Hopkins's striving towards 'The roll, the rise, the carol, the creation'.

is a compelling quality inherent in all his work which draws the reader, if only to leave him gasping, and, perhaps in some cases, sickened. This 'drive', this quality, is the result of a 'single pursuit of . . . an artistic intention', and whether or not this 'artistic intention' is a subordinate one is a matter of little importance here. To my way of thinking, it is not. In much of Dylan Thomas's verse there is a pursuit which never swerves from its intention. The reader may open almost any book, wherever he wishes, and in every case will he be conscious of this intention: he will recognise that 'struggle from darkness towards some measure of light', that 'casting of light upon what has been hidden for too long', that 'naked exposure':

> *I see the summer children in their mothers*
> *Split up the brawned womb's weathers,*
> *Divide the night and day with fairy thumbs;*
> *There in the deep with quartered shades*
> *Of sun and moon they paint their dams*
> *As sunlight paints the shelling of their heads.*
>
> *18 Poems*

> *This world is half the devil's and my own,*
> *Daft with the drug that's smoking in a girl*
> *And curling round the bud that forks her eye.*
> *An old man's shank one-marrowed with my bone,*
> *And all the herrings smelling in the sea,*
> *I sit and watch the worm beneath my nail,*
> *Wearing the quick away.*
>
> *18 Poems*

Here is a searching, a seeing and a discovery. It is the result of an individual struggle, a highly personal conflict, and therefore its general intelligibility is a matter for speculation. Nevertheless it is a manifestation of that singleness of intention, the recurrence and obvious sincerity of which gives a unity to some of Dylan Thomas's best work, and a significance to most of it.

'His intellect, startled at a sight, breaks now into joy, now into inquiry, now into a terror of fearful expectation—but always into song', says Charles Williams, of Hopkins.

In all the poetry of Dylan Thomas one may similarly find two of these elements: inquiry, and a terror of fearful expectation. And, if the first seems a slighter or a more exotic inquiry than that of the God-seeking Hopkins, the latter is intensified to a degree which the secluded Jesuit priest was never conscious of. If there is little joy in the poems of Dylan Thomas, it is because his inquiring, clinical intellect has prohibited it. His probings have laid bare the tumour: his labours 'towards some measure of light' have unearthed those things which are antithetical to a joyous lyricism. Momentarily, he has glimpsed his own origin and end, and, through himself, the origin and end of all men. His problems are theirs; their world his:

> *I dreamed my genesis in a sweat of sleep, breaking*
> *Through the rotating shell, strong*
> *As motor muscle on the drill, driving*
> *Through vision and the girdered nerve.*
>
> *18 Poems*

> *I see the boys of summer in their ruin*
> *Lay the gold tithings barren,*
> *Setting no store by harvest, freeze the soils;*
>
> *18 Poems*

Here can be no easy lyricism, no ringing laughter.

Of the two factors, inquiry and a terror of fearful expectation, there are abundant examples in all Thomas's books. Indeed, it is obvious that without a highly developed capacity for inquiry few of these poems could have been written at all. The poet's consistent and constant desire to uncover what has been too long hidden is itself the proof of his curious nature: and where might a man more commendably start than by inquiring into his own processes, reactions and origins? But the poet does not stop there: his inquiry expands outwards until it embraces the whole system in which man moves; and with this inquiry, again comes criticism:

> *Once in this wind the summer blood*
> *Knocked in the flesh that decked the vine,*
> *Once in this bread*
> *The oat was merry in the wind;*
> *Man broke the sun, pulled the wind down.*
>
> *This flesh you break, this blood you let*
> *Make desolation in the vein.*
>
> *25 Poems*

and also in the whole of the poem, in *25 Poems*, about 'The Hand'.

'Terror of fearful expectation' broods over most of the poems. It is a terror of the darkness, and a fear of hidden things. In bringing these fears into an antiseptic daylight, dragging them into sight and parading them, the poet is teaching himself, and us, to grapple with them, to overcome them.

Often it is the terror of the body, the fear of the self, the powerful black-magic of the subconscious that inspires the poet and disturbs the reader:

> *I dreamed my genesis and died again, shrapnel*
> *Rammed in the marching heart, hole*
> *In the stitched wound and clotted wind, muzzled*

Death on the mouth that ate the gas.
Sharp in my second death I marked the hills, harvest
Of hemlock and the blades, rust
My blood upon the tempered dead, forcing
My second struggling from the grass.

18 Poems

Again it is the terror of man and society; a terror which at last degenerates to a dull nausea and sickness of heart which would have done macabre credit to John Webster:

I have longed to move away
From the repetition of salutes,
For there are ghosts in the air
And ghostly echoes on paper . . .

I have longed to move away but am afraid . . .

25 Poems

Whether this is the desire of the sensitive mind to avoid the torments to which it is subjected by an insensitive society, the desire of the Hermit or the Puritan as protagonist of the Sensualist; or whether it is the longing for death as a release from painful life, the terror is the same, and fear is always there.

I have longed to move away
From the hissing of the spent lie
And the old terror's continual cry
Growing more terrible as the day
Goes over the hill into the deep sea;

25 Poems

(iii)

Apart from such obvious similarities as these quotations have indicated, there are also other factors common to both poets which not only indicate an identity of outlook, but also a strong technical influence by Hopkins on Dylan Thomas.

The first, an identity of outlook, is most apparent in such extracts as the following, where each poet is attempting, by the use of an individual 'clinical' vocabulary, to illuminate some aspects of man. Here is the model:

> Lord of the living and dead
> Thou has bound bones and veins in me, fashioned me flesh,
> And after it almost unmade, what with dread,
> Thy doing. . . .
>
> The Wreck of the Deutschland

This is what Thomas makes of it:

> I sent my creature scouting on the globe,
> That globe itself of hair and bone
> That, sewn to me by nerve and brain
> Had stringed my flask of matter to his rib.
>
> 18 Poems

The important distinction here lies in the difference between *general* and *particular*. Whereas Hopkins is describing the body broadly, as a physical mechanism in contrast to a mental entity, Thomas describes a special part of the anatomy, as he does further, in:

> He holds the wire from this box of nerves.

There is a near-objective treatment in both poets; it is the physical vision elevated into poetry; it is man described as a working model, as a machine; it is the legacy of John Donne.

The emotional rush of words, common to both writers,

and the assonantal and alliterative form which such a rush takes, even exposes them to similar faults, and betrays the blind spot in them both. In Hopkins, this blind spot gives rise to:

Stirred for a bird.

and

Piecemeal peace is poor peace. What pure peace.

and in Thomas, the lesser faults:

Chaste and the chaser . . .

and

Grief thief of time . . .

But conclusive proof of Thomas's derivation from Hopkins lies in the similarity, and very frequently the coincidence of their compound words. There is, in both poets, an abundance of such compounds: the early Hopkins poems seem to owe much to Keats in this respect, but the later ones show an individuality which is nowhere else apparent, save in the poetry of Dylan Thomas.

Frequently the compound words used by the two poets fall into the same fundamental groupings; by which I mean those groupings which are the common heritage of all writers, and which are consequently never original and hence never derivative. Such alliterative compounds as 'May-mess', 'bellbright', (Hopkins), and 'sky-scraping', 'fair-formed', (Thomas), are cases in point.

But when it is found that two poets employ compounds, in which the verbal elements coincide and fall into identical groupings, the deduction is an obvious one. Here, as examples, are: 'moon mark', 'star-eyed', 'sea-corpse', 'bone house' (Hopkins), and 'moon-turned', 'star-gestured', 'sea-faiths', 'bonerail' (Thomas), where the moon-, star-, sea-, and bone-elements are held in common.

This is a major point in the consideration of influences on the work of Dylan Thomas; yet, since it is one which, after the initial statement, may gain little advantage by discussion, I have added an Appendix on the point, in which are gathered together, under certain arbitrary groupings, those compounds which I consider as showing most effectively the one-way commerce between the writers.

COMPOUND WORDS OF HOPKINS AND THOMAS

Class	Hopkins	Thomas
1 Alliterative	May-mess	sky-scraping, fair-formed.
2 Triple-compounds	day-labouring-out	hero-in-tomorrow
3 MAN-	Manshape, man-wolf	Manshape, man-iron
4 Number-compounds	Five-leaved	One-sided, three-pointed
5 WOMB-	Womb-life	Womb-eyed
6 HEART-	Heartsore, heart-forsook	Heartsore, heart-shaped
7 JESU	Jesu	Jesu
8 CHRIST	Christ-done-deed	Christward
9 RE-	Rewinded	Resuffered
10 BONE-	Bonehouse	Bonerail
11 UN-	Uncumbered	Unsucked
12 SEA-	Sea-corpse	Sea-faiths
13 WATER-	Waterworld	Water-clock
14 STAR-	Star-eyed	Star-gestured
15 JACK-	Jackself	Jackchrist
16 MOON-	Moon mark	Moon-turned
17 -Light	Hornlight	Owl-light
18 -Eyed	Star-eyed	Red-eyed, womb-eyed
19 -Tale(s)	Tell tales	Tell-tale
20 -Fathomed	No-man-fathomed	Five-fathomed

CHAPTER FIVE

The Medievalist

(i)

The Romantic realist, and above all, that type of realist who feels remorse at his own realism, is very apt, especially if he has had a Jesuit education, to find a comforting refuge in the conflict between materialism and idealism as it expressed itself in the Middle Ages. We can observe a similar homesickness in Belloc, and even in Chesterton. Such people find in the Middle Ages an echo of their own vitality, their own sense of sin, their own profound conviction of doom. The affinities which exist between a man like Belloc and a man like François Villon and Rabelais are very real affinities. Such an affinity exists also, though in a less conscious form, between the great French realists and Joyce.

It could be well contended that men of intense ethical feeling who become the blacklegs of idealism find in the Middle Ages some solace for, or explanation of, their own conflict. It would not be too farfetched even to indicate how such a temperament finds an outlet in the Rabelaisian love of words—finds in the living language of the streets the pullulating life which is absent from the thin wisps of sophistication which serve for higher culture.

HAROLD NICOLSON 'The Significance of James Joyce' from *The New Spirit in Literature*

To the Medieval mind Hope was the obverse of Fear: the one produced and conditioned the other. The Fear of the devil implied a hope in the power of God; the faith placed in witchcraft implied a corresponding lack of faith in Christianity; the hope of Heaven was offset by the fear of a Hell-fire, the sublime terror of which was possible of adequate description only to such a genius as Dante.

Only that mind, that spirit of the Dark Ages, which could invent the nightmare atrocities of the *Bestiaries* could invest an imaginary animal like the Roman unicorn with such surpassing grace and beauty; or erect, like avenging demons, grinning gargoyles to overlook some of the finest Gothic ecclesiastical architecture that remains to us.

But with the passing of the Middle Ages, it seems that this realisation of hope and fear, as elements of the same feeling, had died in men, or at the least had been greatly diminished when the powers of the witch and the Church passed into other hands. Faith tends to become replaced by fact, and diabolical fantasy by the beginnings of scientific research. Even those writers, belonging to the Modern period of our history, Burton and Sir Thomas Browne, who seem by their use of legend and superstition to be naturally capable of and predisposed to the fantasy and wild explorations of the Middle Ages are, on closer scrutiny, seen to be the precursors of an Age of Reason, who utilise such legends and superstitions for their own elucidatory purposes, and with a degree of scientific detachment unknown at any time before the Renaissance. The hope and the fear are almost lost, and when they do occur later, it is separately, and never to that degree of intensity which marked them in their earlier form.

Almost alone among contemporary writers, Dylan Thomas knew how to recreate within himself a realisation of these factors of Medievalism. Both George Barker and

David Gascoyne have felt and described fear, but seldom
with hope on the obverse; and Thomas's hope was to rid
himself of darkness and the terror of hidden things; his fear
was that of darkness and of hidden things, the most primitive of fears man knows. And as in the case of the Medi-
evalists, to Dylan Thomas, hope implied fear, while fear
proceeded to hope. And above this hope and this fear for
the Self and the world, this terror of and this dragging away
of darkness, broods Death, which grows out of, and is implied in, both hope and fear.[1]

This is what Harold Nicolson calls a 'profound conviction of doom', which is to be observed in those Romantic
realists 'who find in the Middle Ages an echo of their own
vitality', and it is apparent in most of the poems of Dylan
Thomas:

> *I dreamed my genesis in sweat of death.*
>
> *The hand that whirls the water in the pool*
> *Stirs the quicksand; that ropes the blowing wind*
> *Hauls my shroud sail.*
> *And I am dumb to tell the hanging man*
> *How of my clay is made the hangman's lime*

18 Poems

[1] 'The whole poem is haunted by Death ("Atlaswise by owl-light
in the half-way house") (the strangeness is the strange unfriendliness
of and tolerance by Death). The theme treats of the dark soul in the
midst of the death-like state of the modern world:

"The atlas-eater with a jaw for news",

the "half-way house" (which is, now the womb, now the state of the
world, between God and the abyss), the "half-way winds" which
blow the uncertain soul, the space of time between death and the
re-awakening to God:

"That night of time under the Christward shelter".

and the irrevocability of "This mountain minute".'

EDITH SITWELL *Sunday Times* 1936

Black night still ministers the moon,
And the sky lays down her laws,
The sea speaks in a kingly voice,
Light and dark are no enemies
But one companion.

25 Poems

The prophetic invocation of the last line is typical; running close upon the announcement of death's imminence is the possibility of a new lease of life ('O take back this', perhaps a charm against death; a hope). The hope and the fear, like light and dark, are no enemies; they are two sides of the same conflict, that conflict between materialism and idealism which produced the 'Romantic realist'.

Beginning with doom in the bulb, the spring unravels.

War on the destiny of man!
Doom on the sun!
Before death takes you, O take back this.

25 Poems

This conflict between materialism and idealism is also apparent in the juxtaposition of certain words and ideas which separately, would be descriptive of one state or the other solely:

We watch the show of shadows kiss or kill,
Flavoured of celluloid give love the lie,

or,

And from the windy west came two-gunned Gabriel

25 Poems

and,

E

Your corkscrew grave centred//in navel and nipple,
The neck of the nostril.

25 Poems

While at other times the poet is content to use the rhythm
while neglecting the alliteration of such a form:

A steeple-jack tower, bonerailed and masterless . . .
In seizure of silence commit the dead nuisance . . .

As obvious as this use of metre and alliteration is Thomas's
love of archaic words:

'Hold hard', 'My masters', '*From bald* pavilions', '*the*
minstrel *tongue*', 'widdershin', 'unicorn', 'grail'.
Heigh-ho, *the blood and the berry*
And nail the merry squires *to the tree.*

This last example has also the metrical echo of a ballad-
chorus, a feature which is repeated in:

May fail to fasten with a virgin O,

a line which has always reminded me of the chorus:

Gone with the raggle-taggle gipsies, O!

Frequently, one is impressed by an almost indefinable
similarity between words and lines of Dylan Thomas
and passages from more modern ballads with Medieval
themes.

For instance, one is reminded of *La Belle Dame* by these
lines:

> *A merry girl took me for man,*
> *I laid her down and told her sin,*
> *And put beside her a ram rose.*

25 Poems

While these lines bring to mind a distant rhythmic echo of *The Ancient Mariner:*

> *The maggot that no man can kill*
> *And the man no rope can hang*
> *Rebel against my father's dream*
> *That out of a bower of red swine*
> *Howls the foul fiend to heel.*

18 Poems

Perhaps a reference to 'The hanging albatross' in another poem emphasises this association.

Elsewhere Thomas is fond of introducing allusions to certain of the less pleasant elements of Medievalism:

> *Twisting on racks when sinews give way . . .*
> *Strapped to a wheel, yet they shall not break.*

25 Poems

At other times, we are given such images as 'water-clocks' ('The winder of the water-clocks') and 'the pictured devil' (from a tapestry or *Bestiary?*); while everywhere in the poems is that enquiry which is seen sacredly among the Churchmen of the Middle Ages, and profanely among the alchemists and sorcerers. And everywhere in the poems there is that primitive approach, which takes the form of a repetition of superstition and a half-belief in legends:

in *New English Weekly* being singled out years ago by Geoffrey Grigson for special praise.

There are, however, among the poems he published, about a dozen occasions when the poet, standing back just far enough to retain his individuality, gave us something like an objective description of what he saw about him. These poems include, *This bread I break was once the oat, Ears in the turrets bear, The hand that signed the paper felled a city, I have longed to move away,* from *25 Poems; Twenty-four years remind the tears of my eyes* and *The tombs have told me she died,* from *The Map of Love; The Hunchback in the Park* and possibly *In my craft or sullen Art* and *Paper and Sticks,* from work collected in *Deaths and Entrances.* Here there is little of the usual violent conflict of images, but often a clear development of thought rather than of imagery from one point towards another culminating point: and sometimes a concentric and complete development around a central unifying point or image, as in the poem *Paper and Sticks,* where the movement revolves round the fire:

PAPER AND STICKS

Paper and sticks and shovel and match
Why won't the news of the old world catch
And the fire in a temper start.

Once I had a rich boy for myself
I loved his body and his navy blue wealth
And I lived in his purse and his heart

When in our bed I was tossing and turning
All I could see were his brown eyes burning
By the green of a one pound note

I talk to him as I clean the grate
O my dear it's never too late
To take me away as you whispered and wrote

I had a handsome and well-off boy
I'll share my money and we'll run for joy
With a bouncing and silver-spooned kid

Sharp and shrill my silly tongue scratches
Words on the air as the fire catches
You *never did and* he *never did.*

Here the images, adequately profuse as they are, do not
fight or contradict each other, but, growing naturally out of
each other, cause the poem to progress forward as a narrative might do.

Absent from this group of poems are many of the subjective, physical references and images (and also the magic)
that mark the rest of the poet's work. Most of the technical
approaches are dissimilar, a point which may best be
demonstrated by quotation.

Here, first of all, is an extract from a poem which, to my
mind, best illustrates the complex texture of the poet who
has said in explanation, 'A poem by myself needs a host of
images. I make one image . . . let it breed another, let that
image contradict the first, make, of the third image out of
the other two together, a fourth contradictory image, and
let them all, within my imposed formal limits, conflict':

She makes for me a nettle's innocence
And a silk pigeon's guilt in her proud absence,
In the molested rocks the shell of virgins,
The frank, closed pearl, the sea-girl's lineaments.
Glint in the staved and siren-printed caverns,
Is maiden in the shameful oak, omens

is unimpeded by images 'warring among themselves'. Here we may see more clearly the germ from which the finished work has evolved, as in:

> *This bread I break was once the oat,*
> *This wine upon a foreign tree*
> *Plunged in its fruit:*
>
> 25 *Poems*

> *The ball I throw while playing in the park*
> *Has not yet reached the ground.*
>
> 25 *Poems*

Here, to a greater degree than in the rest of his poems, Dylan Thomas is successful in bringing things to the clear light of day, in stripping hidden things of their darkness; for now the problems to be solved are not only those of the poet, but of all men. It is understandable that whenever the poet approaches other problems than his own, his work takes on a new clarity. *The hand that signed the paper, The Hunchback in the Park, Paper and Sticks,* are cases in point. When Thomas is writing clearly in poems involving *himself,* it is usually the case that the problems he treats are common, on an elementary level, to all men:

> *Should lanterns shine, the holy face*
> *Would wither up, and any boy of love*
> *Look twice before he fell from grace.*
> *. . . . let the false day come*
> *And from her lips the faded pigments fall,*
> *The mummy cloths expose an ancient breast.*
>
> 25 *Poems*

To this curious mind, sanity and a temporary peace within himself may only exist when light is cast on all things obscured.

Not only is this antiseptic and near-metaphysical inquiry more apparent in the 'straight' poems; when the poet is less occupied with the functions relatively static within his own body, he is often able to give us with greater clarity and movement images and epithets from the external world.

Not that Thomas's images are even as photographic as those of T. S. Eliot, or Herbert Read. It seems that Dylan is more interested in creating the world to which his personal and often arbitrary images apply than in looking at the existing, visible-to-all-men world and in applying to its phenomena the *mot juste,* as in:

> *They see the squirrel stumble,*
> *The haring snail go giddily round the flower.*

> *The oat was merry in the wind.*

> *And dusk is crowded with the children's ghosts . . .*
>   *. . . . the quiet gentleman*
> *Whose beard wags in Egyptian wind.*

> *25 Poems*

Such is the world, seen as after a long absence spent in internal darkness or an illness, where the movement of a tree is an event, and where the stumbling squirrel makes history. That such event and such history are relatively unimportant, is itself a matter of secondary account in the consideration of the work of Dylan Thomas, which is poetry of its own sort first and last, and only occasionally, and then very generally, propaganda.

(ii)

These poems, partly because of their clearness and straightforward movement, received little adverse criticism,

CHAPTER SEVEN

The Peculiar Contribution of *18 Poems*

ALTHOUGH, as Herbert Read has said, one might regard Dylan's poems as *absolute poetry*, that is, needing no yardstick of time and place to measure them, for the purpose of elementary criticism it is essential to look at them, if ever so briefly, with reference to other work with which we may be familiar.

It is true that *18 Poems* came to us, suddenly and inexplicably; like the bird in the Anglo-Saxon poem, that flew into the lighted room out of the darkness. But before we may understand the delight it brought with it, we must know what manner of flesh and fowl were already in the room, what the mood and situation was like there, which made the advent of such a bird so acceptable.

18 Poems was published by the *Sunday Referee* and The Parton Bookshop, in 1934. It was a well-produced little book, of 36 pages, with a small note by Victor S. Neuburg, Poetry Editor of the *Sunday Referee,* which said: 'This book, the second volume of the *Sunday Referee* Poets Series, is unaccompanied by either portrait or preface, at the author's request.' It appeared quietly and without ostentation, and caused a wordy revolution!

What sort of political and literary house were we living in, in those days, that readers and writers should make so much of this little book? And what were the qualities of the book that they should be so esteemed at this time?

In the world of politics and international affairs, we had seen or were seeing, by 1934, the failure of what our fathers had fought for in the war of 1914-1918, the chaos and distress of the Weimar Republic, the abdication of Alfonso XIII and the bickering in Spain, the beginning of Japan's aggression, Italy's movements towards imperial aggrandisement, the birth of Hitlerism and Germany's unrest, the invalid state of the League of Nations, our own fall from the Gold Standard, and what was regarded as the increasing Russian threat. In a *fin-de-siècle* period of disillusion and disintegration, all political statements were suspect, the Right no less than the Left.

In poetry, there was a similar chaos and depression. It is, indeed, hard at this time of writing to call to mind again the poetic 'situation' of those times. But it went something like this:

Herbert Read's poems hadn't been collected into a volume, Auden's first poems had been published four years before, Spender's had been published one year before. Surrealism was not to be explained by David Gascoyne nor *Murder in the Cathedral* published for another year.

And in 1934, Michael Roberts was, in *Critique of Poetry,* (Cape), still attempting to bring us to T. E. Hulme, who had first become known in 1913, with the Imagist manifesto. Hopkins had appeared four years previously, in 1930.

The Sitwells were still written of as 'Eccentrics'; T. S. Eliot was, according to the *Listener,* 'A Major Critic and a Minor Poet'. And any anthology one picked up would concentrate mainly on W. H. Davies, Harold Monro, Ralph Hodgson, Chesterton, Squire and Blunden; with lots of Brooke and a little Owen.

Among magazines, in America there was *Poetry (Chicago),* and in England, *The London Mercury,* and Mr. Eliot's exclusive *Criterion.*

F

Generally, music-lovers still held up their hands in horror at the mention of Stravinsky: young men wore plus-fours for all outdoor occasions and girls wore Russian boots: Cab Calloway was the dance-band star; and all aircraft were expected to be bi-planes; D. H. Lawrence wasn't to publish *Pornography and So On* for two years; readers of Freud still felt rather daring. Atoms were never mentioned, but Garbo was, incessantly.

It was to this world that a boy of nineteen made public his eighteen poems. How different they were from Mr. Eliot's *Waste Land* depression, W. H. Davies's leisurely perusal of sheep and cows, Mr. Read's Great War reminiscences and Auden's telegraphese. In politics as in literature, there was complete chaos, no way to follow. No standards by which the young man, the young writer, could guide his life or production.

So, Dylan Thomas, thrown back upon himself, produced a poetry of his own, the startling elements of which had never before been combined in the unity of one man's work.

What was his theme? Not the limited countryside, not post-war depression, not Communism, not the beauty of the mechanical world. It was *Man*.

> *And what's the rub? Death's feather on the nerve?*
> *Your mouth, my love, the thistle in the kiss?*
> *My Jack of Christ born thorny on the tree?*
> *The words of death are dryer than his stiff,*
> *My wordy wounds are printed with your hair.*
> *I would be tickled by the rub that is:*
> *Man be my metaphor.*
>
>   *18 Poems*

Or, in paraphrase: 'What am I to write about? Shall it be Death, or love with its bitter-sweetness? Or Christianity?

No, death is as dull as religion, and love is to be suffered not written of. I will write of the most urgent of these themes: Man, from birth to death'.

It seems that no other poet living in 1934 had, without employing incident and situation, written about *Man* so concentratedly. Nor had any poet discussed with such imaginative force his origin and the origins of all men:

> *Before I knocked and flesh let enter,*
> *With liquid hands tapped on the womb,*
> *I who was shapeless as the water*
> *That shaped the Jordan near my home*
> *Was brother to Mnetha's daughter*
> *And sister to the fathering worm.*

18 Poems

This act of carrying poetic description back to the walls of the womb was something quite new in our poetry. However frequently it might have been implied in previous mystic verse, it had never been stated directly.

The element of shock must have been considerable to those readers who could understand the poet's words. A shock which must have been emphasised by the things his poetic language and symbolism allowed him to say: the references to the male organ as: 'A candle in the thighs', 'My father's globe', 'The knobbly ape'. A shock made more complex by the fact that D. H. Lawrence had conditioned the reading-public to love from the *lover's* viewpoint. Here is the result of that love, shown from the suprahuman baby's point of view. But shock isn't the only thing we get from these poems (and most of them are concerned with pre-natal experience). There is a strange magic which we had not heard before running through all the poems, and resulting in passages like these:

I see the summer children in their mothers . .
Divide the night and day with fairy thumbs;
. . . . sunlight paints the shelling of their heads.

As yet ungotten, I did suffer;
The rack of dreams my lily bones
Did twist into a living cipher.

18 Poems

It is a pre-natal magic, so tenderly evoked; the magic of prescience before creation. This 'tenderness' needs some elucidation. It is not the meant-for-grownups tenderness of Kate Greenaway or Mabel Lucie Attwell, whose children are sophisticated dolls, posed and dressed for the delight of adults; nor is it that sort of tenderness provoked by nostalgia, as in Geoffrey Chaucer's dedication of his *Treatise on the Astrolabe,* 'To litel Lewis, my son', where the simple, loving humanity shines back at us through the centuries; still less is it the whimsical and phoney world of Peter Pan or Christopher Robin. But it is a primitive quality, not apparently intended for anyone's delight. It is rather a statement of *qualities* (i.e., the quality of an unborn child's bones, hands, skull-structure, etc.), made objectively—that is, without involving the poet's emotions; though in subjective terms, that is, those terms which come most readily to his mind because of his background and psychophysical equipment.

Elsewhere there is the magic of the sea, the Freudian sea, the womb's waters, that has never left the poet's work:

Sleep navigates the tides of time;
The dry Sargasso of the tomb

18 Poems

(that romantic sea, where nothing is ever lost, but has waited since the beginning of the world to be reclaimed). Or again:

> *And drown the cargoed apples in their tides.*
> *When the galactic sea was sucked*
> *And all the dry seabed unlocked. . . .*
>
> *18 Poems*

And throughout these first poems, there is more than an echo of Blake, who saw the world in a grain of sand, and eternity in an hour: but in Thomas, the sand-grains are cells, that will multiply and make a man, who will populate a world; a reference which occurs even in his most recent work:

> *And yellow was the multiplying sand,*
> *Each golden grain spat life into its fellow,*
> *Green was the singing house.*

And as for seeing eternity in an hour, he senses it with death even while still in the womb:

> *My throat knew thirst before the structure*
> *Of skin and vein around the well*
> *Where words and water make a mixture*
> *Unfailing till the blood runs foul;*
> *My heart knew love, my belly hunger;*
> *I smelt the maggot in my stool.*
>
> *18 Poems*

There is that, in such a quotation, which seems to indicate the poet's concept of completeness before creation, almost of rottenness before ripeness. As Donne said, in a Sermon admired by Dylan Thomas: 'Wee have a winding sheete in our Mother's wombe, which grows with us from our conception, and wee come (are born) to seek a grave'. His world, where death is sensed even before birth, is one in which no progress is possible; where man begins to die as soon as he is brought to life, *or even before that!* Such a concept has the nightmare quality of infinity, and, because it is repressive and retrogressive, is philosophically decadent. It is even a forerunner of the Existentialism of J. P. Sartre, where 'Not to have lived at all is best'! But this is a criticism of Thomas's philosophy, not of his poetry, which is admirable although unhappy.

All this is a poetry of great sensitivity, musical and conceptual: it creates an unsuspected world, for which there is no rightful vocabulary, since it had never before been externalised, yet which Thomas expresses by recourse to ordinary images, twisting and transmuting them to suit his purpose.

In reproducing such an indefinite world, in plotting such unmapped territory, the poet must of necessity proceed by trial and error, which led Geoffrey Grigson to censure Thomas in *New Verse* for using any word as long as it sounded well.

There is an undeniable completeness of form and matter about this book; nor is it apparent from the rest of his work that he has ever improved upon the manner. It is a unique experience which attempts to extend could only debase. It is the sort of thing only one poet can, or should, do— and that only once.

CHAPTER EIGHT

The Poems in *The Map of Love*

T H E S I X T E E N poems which form the first part of the
book, *The Map of Love*, published in 1939, marked
another step in the poet's development.

After the magic and foetal unity of *18 Poems,* Thomas's
second book, *25 Poems,* came as something of a disappoint-
ment to many of his readers. This book seemed to lack the
unified purpose of the first: it gave the impression of being
a poetic scrapbook, in which pieces of different size and
shape, mood and degrees of technical ability were hurriedly
lumped together. Although this book was to be acclaimed by
those admirers who eagerly waited for any manifestation of
the young poet, myself among them, it cannot be denied that,
apart from certain flashes of the earlier Dylan, *25 Poems,*
if not a retrogression, was at least a rather slipshod marking-
time.

Then, three years later, we are given the sixteen poems
of *The Map of Love.* If we could use such statistics to any
true critical purpose, we might say that these poems work
out at five a year, and one over. That is, one poem per ten
weeks, approximately. Ten weeks' inception, shaping and recording should result in work of a high quality! But poets
don't work that way, by the clock or calendar: nor are these
poems of a consistently high standard. Such magnificent
sympathy as *In Memory of Ann Jones,* and such quiet and
touching simplicity as *Twenty-four years remind the tears of*

my eyes, are juxtaposed with the pointless reminiscence of *Once it was the colour of saying* and the turgid and arbitrary *If my head hurt a hair's foot,* where the verbal conceits detract from what might have been a fine situation, almost in the manner of *18 Poems.*

These poems are perhaps more varied in matter and conception than those in Dylan's first book; and more powerful in manner than those of *25 Poems.* They deal variously with the poet's description of his beloved *(I make this in a warring absence . . .),* his announcement, that he has received the call of 'religion' *(It is the sinner's dust-tongued bell claps me to churches),* his grief at the death of an old lady *(In memory of Ann Jones),* his moralising on the fact that he has written little for some time *(On no work of words now for three lean months),* his greetings to his unborn child *(A Saint about to fall),* a conversation between an unborn child and its mother-to-be *(If my head hurt a hair's foot),* and that final poem of this section *(Twenty-four years remind the tears of my eyes),* in which the poet bewails an unheroic future.

There is, as is apparent even from this crude analysis, a widening of Thomas's interests. They even admit the separate existence of others beside the poet, in the persons of Ann Jones and the unborn child. And this is said unmaliciously, since the poet would have been the first to admit that his earlier work had seen other creatures only as an extension of himself. Indeed, that was the only viewpoint tenable if *18 Poems* was to be written with unity. However, the *persona* of the poet is still hovering over his scenes and characters, impregnating them by his personality no less than by his peculiar stock-in-trade of devices. The personality is by turns arrogant and self-pitying, tender and wildly rhetorical: it is never relaxed and unselfconscious, even in a poem like *We lying by sea-sand,* where verbalisms still have too strong a call on the poet's mind to allow him the free lyricism this poem deserves.

The stock-in-trade of technical devices is, like the matter of the poems themselves, varied: there is the magnificent pentameter movement of *Ann Jones*; the rhythmic variety, expressed in long and quite original stanzas, of *How shall my animal. . .* ; and the near-ballad simplicity of *The tombstone told me when she died.* But (and it is frighteningly interesting to note the importance which such trivialities accrue to themselves as one reassesses a poet's work year by year) over all one is conscious of the humourless plethora of sound and deafness:

> *If the unpricked*
> *ball of my breath*
> *Bump on a spout let the bubbles jump out.*

There is the unevocative makeshift imagery, *inorganic* in the movement of the poet's mood and his recording of that mood (I use the word after consideration: Thomas is a poet of *mood* and not of thought. He is perhaps the least intellectual poet of this century):

> *The sharp, enamelled eyes and the*
> *spectacled claws . . .*

> *The supper and knives of a mood . . .*

> *Through the waves of the fat streets nor the*
> *skeleton's thin ways. . . .*

Perhaps most irritating even to the sympathetic reader, is the poet's bare and empty use of such epithets as 'old' and 'bad' and 'ill':

> *forsaken mysteries in a bad dark . . .*

bully ill love in the clouted scene . . .

Shaped in old armour . . .

and his persistence in the employment of slang expressions like 'out of the bum city', 'the gift of the gab'.

One's final impression of the poems in *The Map of Love* is that Dylan had realised the necessity of variety, if he was to continue writing (since progress in any direction was impossible in the *genre* of *18 Poems*), the need for technical development, and the existence of other tones of mind than that of clinical enquiry. But by this recognition did not come the necessary physicking of the poet's over-indulgence in words, a sharpening of his sense of humour (though, as another critic has observed, *as a person*, Dylan was very humorous), care in his use of old or invented epithets or, what is most important in a writer who intends to write about the grandeur and pathos of living, the ability to be humble without being self-pitying, and strong without being self-righteous.

CHAPTER NINE

Deaths and Entrances

THE BOOK of poems, *Deaths and Entrances*, first published in 1946, was remarkable for two reasons: first, it was in effect Dylan Thomas's final poetic statement of importance, and secondly it was the tiniest volume by a living poet to have appeared for half-a-lifetime; the slim volume to end all slim volumes! If it was the publisher's intention to provide a vest-pocket Thomas, he almost succeeded.

Yet the physical size of this book was in no way indicative of its poetic stature. Paradoxically, it was one of the 'biggest' collections of verse of the century, and, looking back rationally over the ten years since its appearance, one might almost say that the only other slim volume fit to stand alongside it was T. S. Eliot's equally emaciated *'Four Quartets'*.

Deaths and Entrances takes its title from John Donne's last sermon, *Death's Duell*, in which he expresses pity for mankind because of humanity's inevitable passing and corruption. It is a naïve point of arrival, or departure, for any cleric or poet, yet when we have stripped down all 'ulterior decorations' and have examined our hearts, we find that it is the point which concerns most of us the most poignantly; the one fact which we cannot run away from—not even with all the facilities of Inter-planetary migration at our disposal. Life passes, and love, which is so closely tied to life, inevitably fades. All the great tragedies have been built on one or the other of these platitudes.

91

The Dylan Thomas of *Deaths and Entrances* was a different man and hence a different poet from the womb-searching obscurantist who wrote *18 Poems, 25 Poems* and *The Map of Love*. Now as a father and a man who had been present when a war was in progress Thomas's awareness of the human condition had been made sharp enough for his poems to cut deeper than ever his theatrically dark adolescent imagination had permitted. The early frenetic excitement and attitudinizing had to a large extent been physicked, and a more profound and satisfying quality had come in its place.

Nevertheless, there were still faults and lest I be accused of critical duplicity I would wish here to reprint what I said in the original edition of this book; yet not so much in self-defence as because the earlier statement contains a catalogue of the appearances of many individual poems, and I cannot now better what I said then:

'At the moment of writing, November 1945, I have been able to discover only fifteen poems[1] by Thomas (apart

[1] The ensuing comments are based only on a reading of the under-mentioned poems:

Poem *(Into her lying down head*
     There were a numberless tongue . . .
     Two sand grains together in bed . . .)
                              Life and Letters To-day November 1940
Poem *(Once below a time . . .)* *Life and Letters To-day* March 1940
Poem *(There was a saviour . . .)*   *Horizon* May 1940
Deaths and Entrances   *Horizon* January 1941
Ballad of the Long-legged Bait   *Horizon* July 1941
Among Those Killed in the Dawn Raid Was a Man
Aged One Hundred   *Life and Letters To-day* August 1941
The Hunchback in the Park   *Life and Letters To-day* October 1941
Request to Leda   *Horizon* July 1942
Vision and Prayer   *Horizon* January 1945
Poem in October   *Horizon* February 1945
Lie Still, Sleep Becalmed   *Life and Letters To-day* June 1945
This Side of the Truth   *Life and Letters To-day* July 1945
The Conversation of Prayer   *Life and Letters To-day* July 1945
In my Craft or Sullen Art *Life and Letters To-day* October 1945

from his film commentary, *Our Country*) published during these five years of war.[1] Three of them appeared in 1940, four in 1941, and one in 1942. There seems then to be a break of two years, and then in January, February, June, July and October of 1945, six poems are published. If my access to material is adequate, and my deductions from that material correct, it seems that this two years' silence is significant: that Thomas completed one phase of poetic development by 1942, and began another about 1945 (though dates of publication can in no way be taken as accurate in the assessment of a poet's development; they are, however, all we have to go on in this case). And, very generally, I would assess these phases as follows: the period up to 1942 marks the gradual decline of the poet's spasm of verbalism, the exit of that plethora of words which grew out of his enthusiasm for his first success, occupying much of *25 Poems* and most of *The Map of Love.* The period beginning with 1945 seems to indicate a new consciousness of the need for technical progression, for religion and humility, and an unambiguous statement of compassion. But over all it marks Thomas's recognition that man must grow older, must become inevitably separated from young things, and must eventually die.

'The adolescent reader might assert that Dylan was never uncertain of that last fact. Nor was he, in the way all young things know death—through fairy-tales and the heart, as a phenomenon that happens to all humanity. But after the age of thirty (doctors, psychologists and biochemists know why) a man comes to look on Death as something that happens to *him*: he is not primarily con-

[1] Since this chapter was written, the volume *Deaths and Entrances* has appeared, containing other poems than those discussed in the first part of this consideration of Thomas's latest work. I prefer, however, to let these words stand as they were originally written.

cerned with a generality like "all humanity". This is a personal, urgent and inescapable fact, known to the head as well as to the heart. And Dylan seems to know that now.

'But the later poems themselves: what are their qualities, and what do they say? It might perhaps be best to take them separately, seeing what elements in each contribute to my conception of Thomas's development.

'Poem (Nov. 1940), *Into her lying down head . . .* is a lover's fantasy, an extravagance of words divided into three sections drawing on such references as King Lear, Queen Catherine, Juan, Circe, Tahiti and Hollywood, to emphasise its amatory character. Such paradoxes as "holy unholy"; such puns as "mourns in the sole night"; such colloquialisms as "the moon rises up to no good", and such a Swinburne-ism as:

> *Damned damned go down or caress to death the sun—*
> *Sized bridal bed's cruellest brood,*

still occur; with a self-echo to the poem in *Map of Love,* "We lying by sea sand", in the second section:

> *Two sand grains together in bed,*
> *Head to heaven-circling head.*

What is most interesting is that the poet, with this poem, seems to have abandoned his hyphenated compound words: "Lying down head", "Once seen strangers". This new departure may, consciously or otherwise, have been due to my calling his attention to his elaborate compounds, about 1938.[1]

---

[1] My comments are on the poem as it appeared in *Life and Letters To-day.* There have been alterations to this poem since.
(a) 'Whales quaked loose from the green grave'
(Life and Letters To-day)
'Whales unreined from the green grave' *(Deaths and Entrances)*

'Poem (March 1940), *Once below a time,* [1] begins with a characteristic schoolboy pun on the fairy-tale opening. Written in irregular stanza forms, with no rhyme, it would pass for bardic buffoonery, but for its last three lines:

> *Now shown and mostly bare I would lie down,*
> *Lie down lie and live*
> *As quiet as a bone.*

The adolescent fury is passing, that is the statement of the young man who feels he is growing up. (Was it all said better in *Twenty-four years remind the tears of my eyes?*) In this poem we are reintroduced to the tailor, the scissor-man, Fate, who sees through all disguises, who, in fact, creates man's disguises.

(b) 'Enamoured Tahiti and shining Hollywood, Circe's
    Swinish, coiling island . . .'   *(Life and Letters To-day)*
    'Man was the burning England she was sleep-walking,
      and the enamouring island . . .'   *(Deaths and Entrances)*
(c) 'Celebrating at his side'   *(Life and Letters To-day)*
    'Celebrating at her side'   *(Deaths and Entrances)*
(d) 'And out of every helled and heavened shell'
                              (Life and Letters To-day)
    'And out of every domed and soil-based shell'
                              (Deaths and Entrances)
The last ten lines of this poem are completely replaced in the later version, but read originally:
    'From the madhouses and menageries
    Of jealous night uncage the grain and bird:
    The love of women and men
    Scrapes and sings denied in them,
Damned damned go down or caress to death the sun—
    Sized bridal bed's cruellest brood,
A man torn up mourns in the sole night.
Betrayed will his love betrayed find an eye or a hair to hate?
Will his lovely hands let run the daughters and sons of the blood?
Will he rest his pulse in the built breast of impossible great God?
Over the world uncoupling the moon rises up to no good.'
Life and Letters To-day

---

[1] Not included in *Deaths and Entrances.*

'Once again, there are references to Nansen and Columbus; there is a deaf internal rhyme,

> *Head, deceived, I believed, my maker;*

there is a transposed epithet,

> *Spiked with a mastiff collar;*

a pun:

> *idol tailor;*

a reference to hire-purchase:

> *Suit for a serial-sum*
> *On the first of each hardship,*
> *My paid-for slaved-for own too late;*

and more avoidance of hyphens: "clock faced tailors".

'Poem (May 1940), *There was a saviour, Rarer than radium,* deals with Childhood's refuge in dreams; the escapism; the escapism, perhaps, of all idealists:

> *Prisoners of wishes locked their eyes*
> *In the jails and studies of his keyless smiles.*

Although there is the regulation pun:

> *near and fire neighbour;*

the customary paradox:

> *his safe unrest;*

this verse is obviously moving towards a new simplicity:

commoner than water, crueller than truth;

says the poet, unambitiously.

'*Deaths and Entrances* (Jan. 1941) is the poet's first work which hints that he might have been writing in wartime:

' "On almost the *incendiary* eve", he begins, and goes on to tell how, in London, his friends and admirers are killed:

> *. . . . . . . friends*
> *Who'd raise the organs of the counted dust*
> *To shoot and sing your praise.*

and how, in the presence of sudden death, one may even come to respect and like one's former enemies.

> *Until that one loved least*
> *Looms the last Samson of your zodiac.*

Once again, in "many married" and "near deaths", the hyphens are omitted.

'Then in July appeared the *Ballad of the Long-legged Bait*; 54 verses, in a rough ballad form, telling what befell when a fisherman used a beautiful young girl as bait. Apart from the references to proper names (Jericho, Biscay, Sheba, Susannah, Lucifer, Venus, and the outsize pun, "Sodom To-morrow"!) this is like no other poem Thomas has published. Its length is tiring; it comes more and more to lack urgency as it progresses, and it seems at the end little more than a technical exercise; but the quality of its sustained fantasy, and its reiteration of the boat-sea relationship, emphasises not only a suspected Freudian

G

symbolism, but also the influence of Rimbaud's *Bateau Ivre*.

'By October 1941, with *The Hunchback in the Park*, we are introduced to what might well turn out to be a foreshadowing of the poet's latest phase. In a poem of seven fairly regular stanzas, we are shown a miserable old man, with a new and almost objective clarity. "A solitary mister", as Thomas calls him:

> *Eating bread from a newspaper*
> *Drinking water from the chained cup*
> *That the children filled with gravel*
> *In the fountain basin where I sailed my ship.* . . .
>
> *Like the park birds he came early*
> *Like the water he sat down*
> *And Mister they called Hey mister*
>
> *The truant boys from the town*
> *Running when he had heard them clearly*
> *On out of sound.*

'It is in such seemingly artless reminiscences that Dylan can score so highly over his contemporaries; and it is when he decorates such essentially simple and moving memories with a festoon of verbal turgidity that his admirers become most despondent about him. In such a poem as this one, he proves beyond doubt that he can see the world outside himself and see it very sharply and sympathetically: yet so often, as in the poem which follows *The Hunchback* in *Life and Letters To-day*, *The Marriage of a Virgin*,

Waking alone in a multitude of loves when morning's light
Surprised in the opening of her nightlong eyes

His golden yesterday asleep upon the iris
And this day's sun leapt up the sky out of her thighs
Was miraculous virginity old as loaves and fishes,

he gives the impression of being a blind man suffering from interminable verbal compulsions.

'*Request to Leda (Homage to William Empson)*, July, 1942, is the last poem to appear before his two years' silence. C. L. Boltz says of this poem, in *Crown to Mend:*

> Thomas himself described the poet's task as discovery, which shows that his own writing was a pouring out of images. But this is only part of the process of creating a work of art. It has to be formed to make it art at all and to make it communicable. Thomas has shown this shaping in his latest work. In July, 1942 a poem of his called *Request to Leda (Homage to William Empson)* appeared in *Horizon*. It consisted of three triplets rhyming *a b a* through every stanza—only two rhymes in all. This careful formation shows Thomas's development.

'In the main, C. L. Boltz is probably right: though it is doubtful whether one learns anything at all useful about the poem in question from the quoted passage. Nor must we suppose that Thomas had never written in a regular stanza form before. One need only go back to *18 Poems* to confirm that.

'What does this new poem look like? Here are the first and third verses:

1

Not your winged lust but his must now change suit.
The harp-waked Casanova rakes no range.
The worm is (pin-point) rational in the fruit.

3

Desire is phosphorous: the chemic bruit
Lust bears like volts, who'll amplify, and strange
The worm is (pin-point) rational in the fruit.

It looks the sort of verse Empson writes: the imagery, "rakes no range", "phosphorous", "volts", "amplify", etc., are the vocabulary of Empson. Dylan is perhaps amusing himself, carrying out a literary exercise in pastiche, intent, like Empson, to provide a verbal jigsaw puzzle for his readers.

'My own judgement is that this is a poetic leg-pull, a trick to call fools into a circle. If it is not, then my feeling is that it is a waste of time to decipher: one must draw the line somewhere.

'And that is the poet's swan-song before his silence. Before I go on to consider the nature of Thomas's latest phase, I would like to quote what Francis Scarfe said about him in 1940 in *Auden and After* (Routledge, 1942):

' "The Bible appears (to him) as a crazy legend, as seen through childish memories of hot-gospelling and the diabolical grimace of the Welsh Bethel . . ."

'And Marshall W. Stearns, an American, writing about him recently, says in *Transformation Three* (Lindsay Drummond):

' "Biblical allusions crowd his poetry and it is evident that his emotions are deeply involved in religious matters, although his references to this subject are likely to be characterised more by rebellion than conformity."

'The impressions one would get from these comments on Thomas's earlier work is that:

(*a*) he regards the Bible (religion) seriously *only as a source of literary material;*

(*b*) he admits religion *only to rebel against it.*

'*Vision and Prayer* was published in January, 1945. It is a Christmas poem about the birth of a child—Christ, one may suppose—and talks as though the poet was an actual witness at the birth. It is a singular poem in that the verses of its first section are printed, as was the fashion among the Metaphysical poets, as diamonds, while the verses of the second section are laid out in the shape of a drinking-glass, perhaps the Communion-cup, or the Grail.

'And what is most remarkable is that, in the fourth verse, the poet confesses:

> *For I was lost who am*
> *Crying at the man-drenched throne*
> *In the first fury of his stream*
> *And the lightnings of adoration.*

While, in the first verse of the second section, he proclaims,

> *I pray . . . .*
> *. . . . for joy has moved within*
> *The inmost marrow of my heart bone.*

and, as this fine poem ends, in a burst of confessional self-abnegation very reminiscent of Francis Thompson's *Hound of Heaven,* says:

> *. . . . In the name of the damned*
> *I would turn back and run*
> *To the hidden land*
> *But the loud sun*
> *Christens down*
> *The Sky.*
> *I*
> *am found*

The opinions expressed by Scarfe and Stearns would seem to apply no longer. The poet has openly accepted God's love, and has rejoiced in his acceptance.

'*Holy Spring*, also published in January, 1945, contains two lines of significance in the poet's present phase:

I climb to greet the war in which I have no heart—

and

. . . I am struck as lonely as a holy maker by the sun.

If one takes the first line literally, then this is the first poem in which the poet has admitted any reaction at all to War; while the second line quoted is a frank confession of loneliness, and, by converse, a movement towards humility, away from arrogance. This is a different poet from the one who once called, proud in his self-sufficiency:

Am I not father too?

'*Poem in October*, February, 1945, continues in this mood of humble supplication:

It was my thirtieth year to heaven,

begins the poet, not only indicating the passage of time, but admitting the goal of his movement through time; and concluding,

> *O may my heart's truth*
> *Still be sung*
> *On this high hill in a year's turning.*

He is praying for another year of life, in the stability of the world he knows, and, what is more, has come to a simple realisation of the heart's truth: a reversal once more of an earlier arrogant defeatism:

> *I have been told to reason by the heart*
> *But heart, like head, leads hopelessly.*
>
> *25 Poems*

This poem is remarkable also for some exquisite allusions to the landscape and activities of childhood; and, perhaps more important still, for a long stanza-form of ten lines, containing a regular pattern throughout the poem of long and short lines of varying rhythms. This technical advance, together with the poem *Vision and Prayer,* marks a definite moving away from the rhythmic monotony of the pentameter line, to which the poet has adhered for so long.

'*Lie Still, Sleep Becalmed* (June 1945) carries on this technical renaissance: it is the nearest Thomas has yet come to the traditional sonnet form. Actually it is a combination of the Elizabethan and Petrarchan modes, having two quatrains and a sestet. He employs half-rhymes in a regular pattern. Although the tone of this poem is one of compassion, its main interest, in the consideration of the poet's development, lies in its continued sea-imagery, possibly his most constant trait, and in "the wandering boat's" association once more with the *Bateau Ivre* of Rimbaud.

'*This Side of the Truth* (July, 1945) is a poem of three regular and technically individual stanzas, addressed to the poet's little son, Llewellyn, who was six years old. In its quiet movement (which, incidentally, calls upon the sea-image yet again), there is a great compassion, a pathos, even a disillusion. It is as though the poet has suffered real grief for the first time, and is focusing his pain on the child he loves:

This side of the truth,
You may not see, my son,
King of your blue eyes
In the blinding country of youth,
That all is undone.

There is here a simple human dignity, which Dylan Thomas had never before fully mastered. There is, moreover, an admission that youth, the youth which the poet spent so prodigally in his verses, is blind, one might say false, to the truth.

'This admission of rhetoric's failure is later emphasised when the poet identifies "rubbish and fire" with "the flying rant of the sky".

'The poem which follows this in *Life and Letters To-day* is appropriately called *The Conversation of Prayer*, and deals with a child going to bed, a sorrowing man and the "love who dies".

'The last poem which I am able to consider is *In my Craft or Sullen Art*, published in October, 1945. It is a short, continuous poem of 20 lines, using a full rhyme, in a subtly-worked scheme. In it, the lonely poet, writing at night, states for whom he is writing. He says:

I labour by singing light
Not for ambition or bread....
      ....I write
On these spindrift pages
.... for the lovers, their arms
Round the griefs of the ages,
Who pay no praise or wages
Nor heed my craft or art,

This is a poem of sympathy with all lovers, and a confessed loneliness, a remoteness, from them. It is almost as though the poet wishes to make an offering to a love which he envies and which he has renounced.

'In it, the poet implies the ephemeral nature of his art ("these spindrift pages"), comparing it with the fundamental sanity, the stability and the tender omniscience of love, described in the lovers,

> *their arms*
> *Round the griefs of the ages . . .*

Is it stretching an analysis too far to deduce that the poet has, at this stage, almost reached his maturity?

'His successive poems have testified to his recognition of a universe outside himself, to his acceptance of religion and his need for prayer. He has accepted the ruling of his heart, has warned his son of the snares of youth: and has, finally, paid his homage to simple lovers.

'Dylan Thomas has moved far from his early self-assurance, his academic view of life and death, and his literary complexity.

'And in this progress he has gained simplicity and increased his stature.

(ii)

'Since I wrote the foregoing words on Thomas's latest work, he has published a further collection, *Deaths and Entrances* (Dent), containing eleven poems which I had not seen in periodicals when they first appeared.

'The results of this book on me are confusing, for whereas, when I considered many of the individual pieces on their magazine appearance, I thought I could detect a ripening and broadening of the poet's art and expression. Now, with those same poems gathered together in a different order, my thesis falls to the ground and the poet assumes once more something like his previous position and stature: and the latter is certainly not what Mr. W. J. Turner termed it in his review of this book, "that of a major poet".

'*Deaths and Entrances* is a collection of unresolved conflicts, which calls to mind Blake's words from *The Book of Urizon*:

> For he strove in battles dire,
> In unseen conflictions with Shapes,
> Bred from his forsaken wilderness,
> Of beast, bird, fish, serpent, and element,
> Combustion, blast, vapour, and cloud.

And one is perhaps even too humorously struck by the "beast-bird-fish" element in Thomas's *Unluckily for a Death*, in such lines as:

> I see the tigron in tears
> In the androgynous dark,
> His striped and noon maned tribe
>   striding to holocaust,
> The She mules bear their minotaurs,
> The duck billed platypus broody in a milk of birds.

Throughout the book one may observe that the poet is forcing himself to take a stand:

> I pray though I belong
> Not wholly to that lamenting
> Brethren. . . . .

even though he is uncertain of the necessity or value of that stand. He is striving with the shapes bred from his own wilderness. And, of course, he is suffering. No man may write well unless he has suffered, and there is that in *Deaths and Entrances* which leads me to believe that the poet has suffered. His mood and expression, for instance, are for the first time *active;* he has lost the passiveness of *18 Poems* and *25 Poems* and is now beginning to move, to take a stand, even though he only half-believes in the position he takes up. Yet this very movement, this progression, is one of limitations, in which the poet does not fend for himself so much as ask the benediction and leniency of God and man:

> *O my true love, hold me . . . .*
>
> *O may my heart's truth*
> *Still be sung*
> *On this high hill in a year's turning.*

It is a poetry of loneliness and fear rather than one of unconquerable endeavour. And there, to my mind, is Thomas's weakness. Another fundamental point of weakness in this latest work lies in the fact that detail and imagery are inadequate to the framework which they are required to occupy. W. J. Turner has enthusiastically hailed Thomas, as I have said, as a "major poet", and it is true that some of the poems in *Deaths and Entrances* create the illusion of great poetry, in that their theme seems vast, and their framework, or form, to be constructed on an heroic scale. But closer inspection reveals that no theme is ever clearly stated and developed from point to point, to its logical conclusion within the poem; and that what is put down on paper is the record of a series of battles and defeats or retreats, each suggesting, but never resolving, the others.

'The lack of attention to epithet ("And down the *other* air and the blue *altered sky* . . ."), the poet's self-inflicted blindness, as it were, as though he did not wish to rein in the rush of his words in order to seek or record the most exact or pictorial description, causes him to note down almost any succession of reasonably musical nouns, which may or may not, according to the luck of the verbal draw, be evocative or carry some semblance of a message, but which, page after page, bounce tinily through the magnificent framework of the poems like peas on a great drum. And the result is an empty rhetoric, a sort of windy eloquence which illuminates nothing, or, as T. S. Eliot observed in "Rhetoric and Poetic Drama" (*The Sacred Wood*, Methuen), "Some writers appear to believe that emotions gain intensity through being inarticulate. Perhaps the emotions are not significant enough to endure full daylight." In this connection, it is interesting to note that in *Deaths and Entrances* the poet uses the unevocative Vocative, "O" or "Oh", 18 times in 59 pages:

> *O Rome and Sodom To-morrow and London . . .*

> *O keep his bones away from that common cart . . . ,*
> etc.

'Without doubting the sincerity which prompted Thomas's poem *When I woke*, there can be no question that the emotion hinted at is something less than significant:

> *Every morning I make,*
> *God in bed, good and bad,*
> *After a water-face walk,*
> *The death-stagged scatter-breath*
> *Mammoth and sparrowfall*
> *Everybody's earth.*

This sort of thing is so fatally easy for any poet to do.

'So much for the general tone of this collection. There are, furthermore, two peculiarities which I feel may be worth mentioning. The first is the poet's increasingly sensitive use of religious imagery, as in "the heron priested shore", and more strikingly in one verse from *A Refusal to Mourn the Death by Fire of a Child in London:*

> *And I must enter again the round*
> *Zion of the water bead*
> *And the synagogue of the ear of corn*
> *Shall I let pray the shadow of a sound*
> *Or sow my salt seed*
> *In the least valley of sackcloth. . . .*

where the poet, not unfamiliar with Welsh Noncomformist severity, as evidenced elsewhere in his work, has in his mind the need for an even stricter adherence and punishment, the possible result of a sense of guilt and a desire for atonement, and a mark of the writer's new concept of responsibility and humiliation.

'Now these factors are necessarily the indications of a spiritual maturity, which I see elsewhere in the poet's new consciousness of floral and vegetable phenomena:

> *a wonder of Summer*
> *With apples*
> *Pears and red currants*

he says, and elsewhere:

> *And the wild boys innocent as strawberries,*

or,

> *Now as I was young and easy under the apple boughs*
> *About the lilting house and happy as the grass was*
> *green. . . .*

This "botanical urge" is a reaction towards a vegetable state, one of inaction and earthy complacence, a contrast between the mutability of human personalities, with their lies and deceits, and the static safety of the botanical world.

'It is noticeable not only in the work of such poets as T. S. Eliot (I am thinking of *Four Quartets*, with its exquisite cherry-tree imagery), Edmund Blunden and the archaeologist Geoffrey Grigson, but also among ordinary human creatures, the non-poets, who solace their lack of artistic creativeness by visits to Botanical Gardens, or, on a humbler scale, by cultivating their allotments and back-gardens.

'Sooner or later, all ordinary men experience a desire to return to the soil, with its known nature and fixed seasons. Only the man who has lived long enough to experience the stupidity and selfishness of his fellows will realise the truth of the advice: "Il faut cultiver notre jardin".

'The earth is man's true ambition and final destiny. And even though, at times, I feel that Lawrence Durrell's description, in *Delta*, 1938, of the Elizabethan might partly apply to Thomas: "their exuberance was so enormous, so volatile, so pest-ridden, so aching and vile and repentant and spew-struck, that here and there, by glorious mistakes, they transcend the canon", in the main, now, I come to see that the poet's real knowledge of the actual world, with its effects on him combining with the effects of time and all its consequent physical and spiritual metamorphoses, are gradually breaking through the terrific barrier of adolescently-attractive visual mechanisms with which he projected his artistic self'.

When I wrote those words, I too was much younger, and it is easy for a young man to cut and thrust without ever noticing that the sandbag might be bleeding.

To-day, in considering *Deaths and Entrances*, I would
have quoted such compassionate and suffering lines as these:

'*The conversation of prayers about to be said*
By the child going to bed and the man on the stairs
Who climbs to his dying love in her high room,
The one not caring to whom in his sleep he will move
And the other full of tears that she will be dead . . .'

'*After the first death, there is no other*'.
                '*And I rose*
            In rainy autumn
And walked abroad in a shower of all my days.
High tide and the heron dived when I took the road
                Over the border
                And the gates
Of the town closed as the town awoke'.

                '*And all your deeds and words,*
                Each truth, each lie,
                Die in unjudging love'.

'*A man torn up mourns in the sole night.*
And the second comers, the severers, the enemies from the
                                            deep
Forgotten dark, rest their pulse and bury their dead in
                                her faithless sleep'.

                '*The dancing perishes*
On the white, no longer growing green, and, minstrel
                                            dead,
The singing breaks in the snowshoed villages of wishes'.

'*Now their love lies a loss*
And Love and his patients roar on a chain'.

*'I climb to greet the war in which I have no heart but
only
That one dark I owe my light . . .
And I am struck as lonely as a holy maker by the sun'.*

Yet I would also have commented on the glory that shines
out behind the suffering in this:

*'O keep his bones away from the common cart,
The morning is flying on the wings of his age
And a hundred storks perch on the sun's right hand'.*

The logical end of such an enquiry as this must be an
examination of the poem, *Fern Hill*, which ends the collection, *Deaths and Entrances*, and which for me is the natural
curtain to this play of poetic development. It is Thomas's
final poetic statement. He has found his refuge in childhood,
always his most convincing territory. When the rushing
years have winnowed the harvest he left behind him, we
shall find no doubt that his truest talent was that of the
Innocent Eye, which showed him unerringly the microcosm
of the child.

Fern Hill is a poem of one mood, and that mood is one
of lyrical ecstasy in the contemplation of childhood seen
from a distance of time. It is a complete evocation of innocence, in pastoral surroundings, without any intellectualised
metaphysic, any probing of the inner darkness, any striving to realise the nature and dimensions of the pre-natal
world. *Fern Hill* shows the clear, clean Paradise of childhood before life becomes vicious and muddied by the tur-
bulent cross-currents of adolescence and of stale time.

The first verse sets the scene; Dylan, the golden, sunlit
child, is happy in the song-filled house in the country. Time
is kind to him. In his imagination, necessarily self-centred

as children are, Dylan feels that he is the master of this
little world; he is lordly, he says, honoured among wagons
and a prince of the apple-trees, which to him are like towns
in which one may live, climbing among them. There are
one or two phrases that need particular mention: *happy as
the grass was green,* which is a charming way of avoiding
the cliché *happy as the day was long*—for the grass *is*
green all day. He does this again in the next verse, with
singing as the farm was home—meaning *always happy,*
for the farm was always home to him and singing denotes
happiness. And again he does it later in the poem with
Happy as the heart was long, which implies that to the
child it seems that happiness will never cease, as long as
life lasts and the heart goes on beating. There is another
verbal trick apparent in the first verse; it is, *Once below a
time,* an old favourite of his. At first sight this seems to be
mere dislocation of a time-honoured nursery phrase, but
actually it is something much more; first, of course, he is
stressing to us that he is telling a tale of childhood—*once
upon a time*—but he is doing something else as well, he is
telling us that all this happened when he was *very* young,
not once *upon* a time, but *below* a time, below the measur-
ing mark, as it were.

The second verse is largely a repetition of the first, as
though Dylan wishes to make sure that we appreciate his
innocent condition then. Instead of *young and easy,* he
gives us the parallel expressions, *green and carefree,* and
tells us now that he was *famous among the barns,* which
balances his earlier description, *honoured among wagons.*
There is also an interesting repetition of the two colours,
green and golden—and *green,* incidently, is used in every
verse. It is a country colour, and this is a pastoral poem. In
this second verse there is also a retrogression to an old
technical trick of his, as old as Anglo-Saxon poetry itself,

H

which Dylan once used with great frequency. It is a tetrameter or four-beat movement with the alliterations balanced on either side of the line:

'And green and golden I was huntsman and herdsman . . .'

Once again in this stanza we are reminded that Time is merciful to the child; though now a new tone enters the poem with the line:

'In the sun that is young once only . . .'

Meaning to say that never afterwards will this golden state of happiness be attained; that it cannot last.

This verse comes to a close on an unusual note for a child, that of religious awareness. Elsewhere the mood is a pagan animal one, but when the poet says:

'And the sabbath rang slowly
In the pebbles of the holy streams . . .'

something new has entered. It is as though the child recognises that this sparkling water is God's handiwork. This of course is the concept which he introduces in the radio script, *The Crumbs of One Man's Year:*

'You could have thought the river was ringing— almost you could hear the green, rapid bells sing in it: it could have been the river Elusina, "that dances at the noise of Musick, for with Musick it bubbles, dances and growes sandy, and so continues till the musick ceases . . ." or it could have been the river "in Judea that runs swiftly all the six dayes of the week, and stands still and rests all their Sabbath." '

With the third verse we have a complete change of movement. The scene having been set and the child's character established, now the poet flies—as lightly as Puck or Ariel—into the mood of almost breathless ecstasy. The words will hardly come fast enough, it seems:

'All the sun long it was running, it was lovely, the hay-
Fields high as the house, the tunes from the chimneys, it
was air

And playing, lovely and watery
And fire green as grass . . .'

The phrases *all the sun long* and *all the moon long,* later on in the verse, are interesting variants of *all the day long* and *all the night long,* actual phenomena like sun and moon being so much closer and more precise to a child's conception than temporal expressions like *day* and *night.* Another phrase worth comment is *fire green as grass*— which can only mean that to the child's vision *grass looks like green fire.* It is a form of transferred epithet.

In this same verse there is also a charming picture, as seen with a child's sharp eye; that of *the hayfields high as the house.* Straightway there comes to one's mind a small cottage backed by a hill on which grows the golden hay. The house must nestle in a hollow—it is the dingle of *The Peaches.* It is the minute and cosy world of childhood again, limited, but spaceless within its limits.

This verse contains one difficulty of interpretation. What are the *tunes from the chimneys?* Could it be birds whistling? They sometimes build in chimney-pots, but usually only in houses where the fireplaces are not used, and Dylan's house seems a lively one. Or could these *tunes* be simply *smoke,* rising and flowing like melodies in the still air? Perhaps the tunes are the sounds made by the wind in the chimney-tops as it sweeps down over the high hayfield at roof level.

I am interested in the poet's words: *I rode to sleep*. Is he dreaming that he is prince of the apple towns on his charger? Or, like the old grandfather in *Portrait of the Artist as a Young Dog*, is he driving off to sleep in an imaginery wagon? Whatever he is doing, the words which follow are splendidly evocative of the fantasy of childhood—in which the simplest and most ordinary things are wonderfully transformed. And so, as Dylan went off to sleep, he thought that the owls and nightjars were flying away with the farm and the ricks!

So far this has been a fairly static verse, but the poet says something at its close which brings speed and even a frightening urgency into it:

'*the horses* flashing *into the dark . . .*'

It is interesting to note that in *The Journey of the Magi,* T. S. Eliot used the same animal to give movement to a quiet passage:

'*And old white horse galloped away into the meadow,*' he says.

Verse four shows us the child wakening from his dream and the familiar pastoral world coming back to him. But observe in what dreamlike terms this reality slowly reassembles itself; for instance, the farm which, you remember, had been whisked off by the owl and the nightjar, now takes on something of the character of a wandering man who has slept out all night. We learn that from the dew on his clothes. The questing, saucy spirit of this man is typified by his familiar, the farmyard cock, which has spent the night out too! Or is it the ghost-defying cock of Celtic myth, whose presence ensures the traveller's return from *under the hill*, from fairyland?

To the child, all this is Paradise itself, the Garden of Eden, where Adam and Eve moved carelessly among green and golden things. To the innocent eye of childhood, then, it even seems a miracle that the sun should come again and grow big and round once more. It is the miracle of creation repeated. Now Dylan sees everything falling into place, as solid and reliable as ever. The friendly clouds clothe the sky and those rascally horses, which flashed away into the darkness as he went to sleep, appear, surprisingly, from their ordinary stables again—though, thinks the observant child, still a little under the spell of the magic night before! And so off they go, onto *the fields of praise*, that is, the green fields which remind us once again of God's goodness and the necessity to give thanks for it.

So, after that climax, the poem begins to draw to its close. We learn that Dylan is also *honoured among foxes and pheasants*, as well as among wagons; that is, he has the complete freedom of the countryside. He tells us again of those new clouds, of his carefree happiness, of the sun coming back again, day after day, and of the high hayfield. But in this verse, we hear for the first time with certainty that this morning ecstasy of childhood cannot last. Now we are told that children must inevitably lose their innocence and grow up.

This point, the loss of innocence, is reiterated in the final verse; *in the lambwhite days*, that is, the innocent days, the child does not think of the solemn world he is later to inhabit. Then follows the highly moving passage in which Time, who had always been so kind, takes the boy's shadow by the hand and leads him up to the swallow-thronged loft at night. I interpret the shadow to mean that this is not the child we knew before; it is a changed boy, a shadow of what he had been. He is growing up, away from his other self. Time shows him the swallows in the loft, and they are birds of passage who gather before flying away. In this case they are the symbols of Dylan's innocence, which is about to fly away, for the summer of childhood has gone.

And soon the child will wake, not to a Paradise of hay-fields and streams, but an ordinary workaday grey farm, all its magic gone. The land will be childless; that is, childhood will have left the dingle.

This poem ends with a pathos that I do not find equalled in any other poet, save perhaps John Donne, and that principally in the Sermon which I have mentioned before:

> 'Wee have a winding sheete in our Mothers wombe, which grows with us from our conception, and wee come to seeke a grave; and as prisoners discharge'd of actions may lie for fees, so when the wombe hath dis-charged us, yet we are bound to it by cords of flesh, by such a string, as that we cannot goe hence, nor stay there; wee celebrate our own funeralls with cries, even at our birth'.

Dylan Thomas puts the same idea differently:

> *'Oh, as I was young and easy in the mercy of his means, Time held me green and dying'.*

But he concludes the idea with an even greater force than did John Donne, in his most moving line:

> *'Though I sang in my chains like the sea'.*

Perhaps I should point out that here the poet's intention of meaning is: 'Though I sang, like the sea (naturally, endlessly, like my namesake) in my chains—the inevitable binding to the sad situation of the world, by which the child at last must lose his carefree innocence'.

CHAPTER TEN

Faults and Function

IT IS TRUE, and it would be fatuous to pretend otherwise, that Thomas's poetry has its faults: there are the *ad nauseam* repetition of personal stylisms ('death's feather', 'decked with flesh') of imagery (particularly the 'sea' image), the untwisting and mutilation of proverbial phrases ('my camel's eye will needle'), the cosmic joking and the numerical conceits. Yet they are the personal idiosyncracies of the poet, which must be accepted if his work is to be accepted at all. They are individual elements of his peculiar technique: prohibit them, and the sudden, surprising *éclat* of his poetry vanishes.

Distasteful to some readers must be the poet's immense violence, his wild, tempestuous 'madness', with its paradoxical imagery, its amusing vanity and its schoolboy puns. Thomas's poetry, said Hugh Gordon Porteus terribly many years ago, 'is like an unconducted tour of Bedlam', and then went on to hazard the opinion that had Thomas been born an Elizabethan, he would have been another Webster.

It is this 'madness' which has caused Thomas to be lumped together with the Surrealists. Spender, writing impossibly long ago in the *Daily Worker*, said, 'The truth is that Thomas's poetry is turned on like a tap; it is just poetic stuff with no beginning nor end, or intelligent and intelligible control'. To which Thomas very appropriately replied, in a letter to me, 'My poems are formed: they are watertight compartments. Much of their obscurity is due to rigorous compression; the last thing they do is to flow; they are much rather hewn'. It seems to me that the real answer lies somewhere between these two statements: that whereas the initial imagery might be achieved with some labours, the later images might produce themselves in a rush of musical association after the first prompting. In which case, Thomas's obscurity would be due less to rigorous compression than to its opposite, and to the elementary fact that his associations are not necessarily those of his readers. The converse will be true also, in many cases, that the first images, the motivating germ or spontaneous 'inspiration', will occur automatically, to be followed later by a conscious hewing of images which will best suit the poem's opening.

There is, further, the possibility that Thomas's special form of obscurity was in part produced by an inability or lack of desire to shake off his duality and to conceive himself as being one unit of a reality: he was, like Tiresias, both the lover and the loved, existing at one time on different, impinging planes:

I, in my intricate image, stride on two levels,
Forged in man's minerals, the brassy orator
Laying my ghost in metal,
The scales of this twin world *tread on the double,*
My half ghost *in armour hold hard in death's corridor,*
To my man-iron sidle. . . .

25 Poems

Elsewhere, he said, further supporting this view that he was unable, or did not wish, to orientate himself, to exist as one personality:

Am I not father, too, and the ascending boy,
The boy of woman and the wanton starer
Marking the flesh and summer in the bay?
Am I not sister, too, who is my saviour?
Am I not all of you by the directed sea
Where bird and shell are babbling in my tower?
Am I not you who front the tidy shore,
Nor roof of sand, nor yet the towering tiler?

25 Poems

In a letter to me he said: 'I hold a beast, an angel, and a madman in me, and my enquiry is as to their working, and my problem is their subjugation and victory, downthrow and upheaval, and my effort is their self-expression'.

Connected with this insecurity of identity, and so further responsible for his 'difficulty', was the poet's multiplicity of conflicting emotions, and their variety of statements. Here, it seems, he may be suffering from a deficiency which T. S. Eliot has noted in *Hamlet and His Problems:*

> The only way of expressing emotion in the form of art is by finding an 'objective correlative'; in other words, a set of objects, a situation, a chain of events which shall be the formula of that *particular* emotion; such that when the external facts, which must terminate in sensory experience, are given, the emotion is immediately evoked.

Hamlet, thinks Mr. Eliot, is unable to find that 'objective correlative' which would enable him to express clearly his emotions. Hence his 'madness', his levity and punning buffoonery, which are a form of emotional relief. It is perhaps not too much to say that Dylan Thomas, with his spasmodic violence, his brooding terror, and his warring images, is seeking this same 'objective correlative' and, failing to find it, was indulging in his own form of emotional relief. His problem may even have been that of Hamlet. But, in any case, it is that major problem of every man of sensibility. Am I to strive towards some measure of Godhead, or am I to guide, and be contented with, myself as I am?

In the drunken Godhead of adolescence, he was, necessarily for a Romantic poet, fond of the dramatic gesture, which flowed from him in the form of a mouthful of fine words. He rolled them on his tongue as a lesser spirit might roll a wad of chewing gum, and as easily. These words were born of a desire for magnificence, sired by Sense of Glory out of Innocent Eye. It was the same sense which so often caused him to introduce the names of heroes (Caesar, Nansen, Blake) into his lines. The naming of heroes has been an early habit of many more poets than Thomas; Shakespeare and Auden were addicted to it once.

A variant of this capacity for rhetoric is seen in such a passage as this, from *The Map of Love:*

> *If my head hurt a hair's foot*
> *Pack back the downed bone.*
> *If the unpricked ball of my breath*
> *Bump on a spout let the bubbles jump out.*

which appears to be the result of a verbal compulsion, a musico-rhythmic automatism which, once started, will not be reined, whatever the labyrinthine nonsense it may produce.

It is true also that the poet had a limited vocabulary, and that he made one word serve many purposes of meaning, so producing obscurity because we were not always sure of the particular connotation he attached to the word in the particular instance which concerned him. Alas, *Scrutiny!*

Moreover, and more reprehensibly, Thomas often allowed his poetic high-spirits to let him 'doodle' verbally on the page, producing a pattern of sounds, a musical exercise, a bit of word-juggling:

> *Now*
> *Say nay,*
> *Man dry man,*
> *Dry lover mine*
> *The deadrock base and blow the flowered anchor,*
> *Should he, for centre sake, hop in the dust,*
> *Forsake, the fool, the hardiness of anger.*
>
> *25 Poems*

This sort of teasing irritates most severely when it occurs alongside a passage of clarity, or on an occasion when the reader has already been caught up with the 'magic' of the poem concerned. This is especially the case when Thomas chose for himself a difficult way of saying something essentially simple, or when, by his music and rhetoric, he magnified a triviality; and he seemed naturally apt at times to make a tremendous pronouncement of something that was essentially commonplace, just as an intoxicated man might do:

> *When it is rain where are the gods?*
> *Shall it be said they sprinkle water*
> *From garden cans, or free the floods?*
>
> *25 Poems*

Yet, having said that, one has said enough. Julian Symons went on a stage too far in his criticism when he wrote: 'What is said in Mr. Thomas's poetry is that the seasons change: that we decrease in vigour as we grow older; that life has no obvious meaning; that love dies. His poems mean no more than that. They mean too little'.

One agrees that this is what Thomas's poems mean, in the main; but that is not too little for poems to mean. Indeed, it is a great deal for them to mean, if one is to believe Shakespeare and Browning and Tennyson and Donne and Keats—almost everyone else save, perhaps, Julian Symons.

Of course, Dylan Thomas was his own worst enemy, in that he played into critical hands with a sublimity matched only by his resilience after an attack. His method is based on the statement of an elemental truth in his first stanza, and the restatement of this same truth with appropriate variations in succeeding verses. That is, he makes known his thesis, and then proceeds to reiterate without development but in different words, a process which can best be seen at work in the poem, *The Force that through the green fuse drives the flower,* from *18 Poems.*

But Dylan Thomas was a Dog among the Fairies; that is, a cataclysmic force among poets deadened by tradition or political barbiturates. His choking verbalisms, his fixations on certain threadbare or obscure epithets, his inability to resist certain inorganic alliterations, his wilful obscurity, his deafness to certain poor rhymes, his rhythmic monotony, his careless use of words, the over- or under-stress occasioned by his rhetorical mechanisms, his uncertain arrogance—all these are evidence of his rebellion; evidence also that he wrote impulsively, almost automatically, instinctively, his technique conditioned by habitual verbalisms, and initially *for his own benefit,* to strip things clean, as he said. One can hardly picture him as being concerned by the image of a possible reader of his work.

Yet it is this very quality which must inevitably prevent him from being a philosophic influence on any succeeding generation; he did not think, he wrote as he wished. His contribution to poetry must therefore be a technical one only.

And who, without his personal problems, would need Thomas's specialised technique for the writing of verses? There could be few.

Nevertheless, in his day, Dylan Thomas was a necessary antidote to those poets who were different from him—Auden and MacNeice and Day Lewis, for instance, at least one of whom has since on occasion imitated Thomas. Moreover, he was, in his unbalance, a balancing factor to those arid translators, such as John Heath-Stubbs, for whom the sudden flash of fire and the bright scene mean nothing.

And when all is said, what is it that truly matters in a poet? That he should be human, can be the only answer; and Dylan Thomas was that.

CHAPTER ELEVEN

Some Comments On The Prose

(i)

THE NARRATIVE prose writings of Dylan Thomas seem to fall naturally into two groupings: those which were first included in *The Map of Love* (1939) and those of *Portrait of the Artist as a Young Dog* (1940). These two books were rather focal points than definitive collections. That is, Thomas had written other tales in the same genre as those of *The Map of Love*, though he did not collect them; and again, both his radio reminiscences and such a late story as *The Followers* (first published in *World Review,* October 1952) clearly belong to the mood and even the expression of *Portrait of the Artist.* Which means that for all essential purposes what the prose-writer Dylan Thomas had been in 1940 was what he was in 1952. Indeed, it is a defensible critical opinion that even his latest work, *Under Milk Wood,* adhered organically to the *Portrait* period—however far that may have been before 1940—and allowing for the fact that in *Portrait* he is re-living his Swansea boyhood and in *Milk Wood* evaluating Laugharne and New Quay, towns of his manhood, in the same terms.

The obvious conclusion is that Thomas the Prose did not travel very far, even though he crossed the Atlantic a number of times. For him, Laugharne at twenty was an exten-

sion of Swansea at fifteen; and New York at 39 must have
been pretty much like anything else he had known in his
schooldays. He was concerned with the human idiosyncracy
of any place he lived in, and men are not so very different,
whatever they call their cities, at the level of the heart.

Dylan Thomas's earliest prose work was dark, carnal and
'poetic'; rather like *18 Poems*, but less 'finished' because
less *contained*, as a 'watertight column of words' on a single
page.

The first of his stories I recall reading was *The Burning
Baby*, a wild and nightmare reconstruction based on the
historical character, Doctor William Price of Llantrisant,
who died aged 93 in 1893 and who was the pioneer of
cremation in Britain. This Doctor Price, a man of great
intellect, a political exile in France after the 1839 Chartist
riots, was a proclaimed pagan who called himself a Druid,
dressed in a fox skin, named one of his sons Jesus Christ
and, chanting strange laments, burnt his dead body in
paraffin on Llantrisant hill.

Such a twilit tale would naturally appeal to the youthful
Byronism of Dylan Thomas, who celebrated it in his own
manner, with the burning child crying out at the end, word-
lessly as the sharp flames licked about him.

Other stories of the same period, *The School for Witches*
and *The Holy Six*, appeared in Roger Roughton's little
magazine, *Contemporary Poetry and Prose*, during 1936
and 1937. The formula could not have been very palatable
to many over twenty. In the first tale there were found
veins hardening in breasts, fingers hardening on light, and
blood striping 'the thin symbols of fertility'. The mystic
numbers three and seven occur incessantly and an obscure
scissorman materialises among the thirteen dancers in the
inner rooms of Cader House. Yet the end of the strange
melange had power:

'Mr. Griffiths, half blinded by the staring of the moon, peeped in and saw them. He saw the newborn baby on the cold stones. Unseen in the shadow by the door, he crept towards the baby and lifted it to its feet. The baby fell. Patiently Mr. Griffiths lifted the baby to its feet. But the little mandrake would not walk that night'.

In *The Holy Six* (principally important for its introduction of the word *Llareggub*, a place still named in *Under Milk Wood*, though spelt slightly more acceptably as a backwards puzzle) we have a woman who drifts in a maze of hair and touches a rector 'in a raw place'. This piece is full of slant eyes, blood, full breasts and fur feet. Cocks crow, sheep cry, the wood burns 'like cantharides', and the final impression is of a very young, but very verbally-active writer.

A quotation from this tale will show that Thomas had already found the note which he was to strike thenceforward with major variations:

'The world, for him, rocked on a snapped foot; the shattered and the razor-bedded sea, the green skewered hulk with a stuffing of eyes, the red sea socket itself and the dead ships crawling around the rim, ached through the gristles and the bone, the bitten patch, the scaled and bubbling menses, the elastic tissues of the deep, the barbed, stained, and scissored, the clotted-with-mucus, sawn and thorny flesh, ached on a never-ending ache'.

This was published in 1937. In 1943 the *Rabelaisian List* was still the most important ball in the Welsh Juggler's conjuring-kit, though its colour faded as the years built up:

I

'I was born in a large Welsh industrial town at the beginning of the Great War: an ugly, lovely town (or so it was, and is, to me), crawling, sprawling, slummed, unplanned, jerry-villa'd, and smug-suburbed by the side of a long and splendid-curving shore where truant boys and anonymous old men, in the tatters and hangovers of a hundred charity suits, beachcombed, idled, and paddled, watched the dock-bound boats, threw stones into the sea for barking outcast dogs . . .'

Reminiscences of Childhood

In 1952 he was still saying:

'We walked towards the Marlborough, dodging umbrella spokes, smacked by our windy macs, stained by the steaming lamplight, seeing the sodden, blown scourings and street-wash of the town, papers, rags, dregs, rinds, fag-ends, balls of fur, flap, float, and cringe along the gutters, hearing the sneeze and rattle of the bony trams and a ship hoot like a fog-ditched owl in a bay. . . .'

The Followers

There is little difference in the approach, though the themes become more vertebrate as time goes on.

However, in general, the stories collected in *The Map of Love*, belonged to Thomas's early period. But that is not to imply inadequacy of any sort. One of them at least, *The Visitor*, which records a man's grave illness, is superbly ended:

'Rhianon, he said, hold my hand, Rhianon.

She did not hear him, but stood over his bed and fixed him with an unbreakable sorrow.

Hold my hand, he said. And then: Why are you putting the sheet over my face?'

After that, *Portrait of the Artist as a Young Dog* must have come almost as an anti-climax to Dylan's Intense Followers; yet in its everyday reminiscence of childhood, we must agree that Thomas is growing up to an acceptance of the necessity to appeal (as Dickens, and Tennyson and Scott did before him) to the average intelligent middle-aged reader—those who bought the books, not those who raved over library copies.

There are two passages from *Portrait* which are appealing in their different ways. The first shows Thomas's acute awareness at last that a character must be drawn, in the Dickensian sense, if he is to be believed:

' "Whoa there, my beauties!" cried grandpa. His voice sounded very young and loud, and his tongue had powerful hooves, and he made his bedroom into a great meadow. I thought I would see if he was ill, or had set his bed-clothes on fire, for my mother had said that he lit his pipe under the blankets, and had warned me to run to his help if I smelt smoke in the night. I went on tiptoe through the darkness to his bedroom door, brushing against the furniture and up-setting a candlestick with a thump. When I saw there was a light in the room I felt frightened, and as I opened the door I heard grandpa shout, "Gee-up!" as loudly as a bull with a megaphone.

'He was sitting straight up in bed and rocking from side to side as though the bed were on a rough road; the knotted edges of the counterpane were his reins; his invisible horses stood in a shadow beyond the bed-side candle. Over a white flannel nightshirt he was wearing a red waistcoat with walnut-sized brass buttons. The over-filled bowl of his pipe smouldered among his whiskers like a little, burning hayrick on a stick. At the sight of me, his hands dropped from the reins and lay blue and quiet, the bed stopped still on a level road, he muffled his tongue into silence, and the horses drew softly up.

' "Is there anything the matter, grandpa?" I asked, though the clothes were not on fire. His face in the candlelight looked like a ragged quilt pinned upright on the black air and patched all over with goat-beards.

'He stared at me mildly. Then he blew down his pipe, scattering the sparks and making a high, wet dog-whistle of the stem, and shouted, "Ask no questions".

'After a pause, he said slyly: "Do you ever have nightmares, boy?"

'I said: "No".

' "Oh, yes, you do", he said.

'I said I was woken by a voice that was shouting to horses.

' "What did I tell you?" he said. "You eat too much. Whoever heard of horses in a bedroom?" '

The incident and the character come immediately off the page. At last Thomas had learned how to make prose obey his objective purpose.

The second quotation from *Portrait of the Artist*, a gem of its kind, shows a superb mastery of that gossamer territory of boyhood in which time stands still and a tussle with a barn-door may become in retrospect as fearsome as any meeting with a Miura bull at five in the afternoon: it comes from a story called *The Peaches:*

'Jack went skulking into the damp dingle, his hands in his pockets, his cap over one eye. I left the collie sniffing at a mole-hill, and climbed to the tree-top in the corner of the lavatory field. Below me, Jack was playing Indians all alone, scalping through the bushes, surprising himself round a tree, hiding from himself in the grass. I called to him once, but he pretended not to hear. He played alone, silently and savagely. I saw him standing with his hands in his pockets, swaying like a Kelly, on the mud-bank by the stream at the foot of the dingle. My bough lurched, the heads of the dingle bushes spun up towards me like green tops, "I'm falling!" I cried, my trousers saved me, I swung and grasped, this was one minute of wild adventure, but Jack did not look up and the minute was lost. I climbed, without dignity, to the ground'.

Even the punctuation, in which Dylan was usually so traditionally meticulous, seems to have taken fright at the occasion, and to express the urgency of that humiliating fall-that-never-happened!

The Followers, an example of Thomas's last narrative work, is to all intents and purposes the same sort of thing over again, though he sets the autobiography in early adolescence, to tell how he and a friend go out one wet night to follow a girl home, for no other reason than that they have nothing else to do. The girl goes to a humble little house, where her ordinary mother cooks her supper. The boys watch through the lighted back-window in the rain. At this point the two women fetch out an old family photograph album—and then the story takes another turn. It sloughs off its ordinariness and moves so smoothly into the supernatural that one is left astounded.

And one's astonishment is really one's realisation that Young Dylan is now the master of the dark Gods which once took control of his pen, only eighteen years before, when he wrote *The School for Witches*.

Now he has learned to drag them outside, on a wet night, and make them gibber to the time he beats.

(ii)

The radio prose of Dylan Thomas is alternately trivial and important; trivial in that it so often depends on the slick line:

> *'Jaunty girls gave sailors sauce'.*
> *'The groves were blue with sailors'.*

and the recherché literary comment:

> 'Smoke from another chimney now. They were burning their last night's dreams. Up from a chimney came a long-haired wraith like an old politician. Some-one had been dreaming of the Liberal party. But no, the smoky figure wove, attenuated, into a refined and precise grey comma. Someone had been dreaming of reading Charles Morgan'.
>
> *Quite Early One Morning*

or again:

> 'The man who begins a story for a girl's popular weekly—"Myrtle's" or "Pam's", or maybe it is "Greta's" now, or "Ingrid's"—with a subtle analysis of the state of mind of a neurotic young man of letters about to meet a phobia, socially, in a disused Nissen-hut, will never make the grade and is doomed to per-petual immurement in magazines with a circulation of seventeen poets and a woman who once met Kafka's aunt'.
>
> *How to Begin a Story*

trivial in that the writer seems to set too great a store on his puns, one of which seems to strike him so favourably that he uses it more than once:

'men from the B.B.C. who speak as though they had the Elgin Marbles in their mouths'

'Ulterior decorators'

'Sworded Ukrainians—I mean, Ukrainians with swords —leap and kick above the planted sea'

And trivial, or perhaps the kinder word is *slight*, in that it shows Thomas the Critic was no great expert, despite what has been said by a few of his *aficionados*, that his knowledge of literature was immense and detailed. Indeed, in his literary broadcasts Thomas breaks no new ground, but seems content merely to retail average comment, and works himself up into a state of enthusiasm only when he talks about warriors, such as Wilfrid Owen and Sir Philip Sidney (parts of that boyish Hero-cult which is indicated in the poems by his use of names like *Caesar* and *Blake* and *Nansen*); a common trait among critics whose health prevented them from joining the Army.

Yet there are many things in the book of radio scripts, *Quite Early One Morning*, which one is glad to have in print. His immense and open-handed sense of fun finds its right note when he becomes the satirist of contemporary literary forms:

'Then there is the story of rural life. . . . I mean the kind of story set in a small, lunatic area of Wessex, full of saintly or reprehensible vicars, wanton maidens, biblical sextons, and old men called Parsnip or Dottle.

'Let us imagine a typical beginning:

' "Mr. Beetroot stood on a hill overlooking the village of Upper Story. He saw that there was something wrong in it. Mr. Beetroot was a retired mole-trapper. He had retired because he had trapped all the moles. It was a fine winter's morning, and there were little clouds in the sky like molehills. Mr. Beetroot caught a rabbit, taught it the alphabet, let it go, and walked slowly down the hill".

'There we have firmly fixed the location and mood of the story, and have become well, if briefly, acquainted with Mr. Beetroot, a lover of animals and addicted to animal education'.

How to Begin a Story

In embryonic form, Upper Story might almost be the crazy town under Milk Wood, and Mr. Beetroot the poet himself.

Indeed, these radio scripts frequently reach out beyond themselves into other work by Thomas, illumining another concept or poetic image. In the poem *Fern Hill*, for example, Thomas says:

> *And the sabbath rang slowly*
> *In the pebbles of the holy streams.*

while in *The Crumbs of One Man's Year* he tells us:

'You could have thought the river was ringing— almost you could hear the green, rapid bells sing in it . . .'

'He was a long time dying on the hill over the star-lit fields where the tabby river, without a message, ran on, with bells and trout and tins and bangles and literature and cats in it . . .'

At other times in the radio scripts one is pulled up with a jolt by some curiously repeated idea. In *Holiday Memory* we have:

> 'And two small boys fought fiercely and silently in the sand, rolling together in a ball of legs and bottoms'.

while in *The Crumbs of One Man's Year* we are given a similar picture of silent, savage concentration:

> 'Discourteously I shone my torch. There, in the thick rain, a young man and a young woman stood, very close together, near the hedge that whirred in the wind. And a yard from them, another young man sat staidly, on the grass verge, holding an open book from which he appeared to read. And in the very rutted and puddly middle of the lane, two dogs were fighting, with brutish concentration and in absolute silence'.

As a conclusion to a radio talk, this must have had an unnerving effect on listeners. Such an image would go on working in the listener's mind long after the voice which spoke the words was silent.

And it is in this same script that Thomas provides us with a quite unparalleled picture of his own almost unfocussed and generalised poetic self—that self which was so often responsible for poetic vagueness and repetition, an almost somnambulistic state, sensitive in the extreme, but relaxed and imprecise:

> 'I was walking, one afternoon in August, along a river-bank, thinking the same thoughts that I always think when I walk along a river-bank in August. As I was walking, I was thinking—now it is August and

I am walking along a river-bank. I do not think I was thinking of anything else. I should have been thinking of what I should have been doing, but I was thinking only of what I was doing then and it was all right: it was good, and ordinary, and slow, and idle, and old, and sure, and what I was doing I could have been doing a thousand years before, had I been alive then and myself or any other man. . . . There were trees blowing, standing still, growing, knowing, whose names I never knew. (Once, indeed, with a friend I wrote a poem beginning, "All trees are oaks, except fir-trees"). There were birds being busy, or sleep-flying, in the sky. (The poem had continued: "All birds are robins, except crows, or rooks"). Nature was doing what it was doing, and thinking just that. And I was walking and thinking that I was walking, and for August it was not such a cold day'.

The piece ends with Dylan dragging to the river-bank with a stick a scrap of old, sodden paper, which he reads with difficulty. It states that 'over a hundred years ago, a man in Worcester had, for a bet, eaten, at one sitting, fifty-two pounds of plums'.

No man who could write like that would let the world hurry him.

(iii)

Under Milk Wood, A Play for Voices, is perhaps Thomas's most perfected piece of work. It possesses the organic unities of time and place. Its three Acts are morning, noon and night; its setting, a crazy town; its characters, the population of that town, dead and alive—blind Captain Cat, the Rev. Eli Jenkins, Polly Garter, Gossamer

Beynon, and a score more, each one a zany, yet each one a quintessential prototype, rather like characters from a rustic Ben Jonson or perhaps like those of a less sophisticated *Spoon River Anthology*, a work which Dylan Thomas admired.

He liked small towns, mad towns, where the foibles of ordinary men and women were more exposed than they could have been in the anonymity imposed by a big city. In his Preface to *Under Milk Wood*, Daniel Jones tells us that Thomas had such a 'play' in mind for some time. He had long projected a work called *The Town Was Mad*, in which the eccentric townsfolk on trial learn of the pattern of urban sanity—and then 'beg to be cordoned off from the sane world as soon as possible'.

The parallel which suggests itself is, of course, that of the Wise Men of Gotham, those sly ones of legend who evaded a beggaring royal visit by feigning such mad antics as raking the cheese-moon from the village pond and by attempting to pen in the cuckoo by building a stockade about the tree in which he sang those notes which they professed so ardently to admire.

It is perhaps of minor interest that Thomas himself once took part in a gramophone recording in which he was one of these Wise Men of Gotham.

It seems to have been a theme which appealed to his naturally rebellious mind, and he had already, in 1945, broadcast a talk, *Quite Early One Morning*, in parts of which the essential germ of his *Play for Voices* is discernible:

> 'I am Captain Tiny Evans, my ship was the *Kidwelly*,
> And Mrs. Tiny Evans has been dead for many a year.
> "Poor Captain Tiny all alone," the neighbours whisper,
> But I like it all alone and I hated her. . . .

Open the curtains, light the fire, what are servants for?
I am Mrs. Ogmore Pritchard and I want another
  snooze.
Dust the china, feed the canary, sweep the drawing-
  room floor;
And before you let the sun in, mind he wipes his shoes'.

But the keenly observed, Lear-like fools of *Under Milk
Wood* are so appealing that one weeps both for and with
them, even as one laughs—for their poor frailties, their
petty problems and their exposed private tragedies are those
of the world in miniature, but revealed in so concentrated
a miniature as to twist a knife in the heart of pity with every
sentence. They are men and women in the grip of little
lusts, of impossible yearnings, of the grey monotonies of
small towns; simple souls—or crafty ones only as dumb
creatures must be crafty, to survive—who speak their hopes
and despairs within a formal pattern of constantly shifting
repetition, until in the end their trivial lives are magnified
to such size and dignity that we sense in them the nature of
all mankind. Once more, as in his best poems, Thomas
reduces multitude to a unity of effect, sees the world in a
grain of sand, and leaves us wet-eyed to share his vision.

The kindly satirical observation and characterisation of
Under Milk Wood are superb; but it is perhaps in the
humour and warm pity of the play that Thomas shows
his most moving step forward from the earliest arrogant
obscurity.

The chorus of dead sailor comrades speaking in the head
of blind Captain Cat have the stuff of great tragedy in their
ordinary words:

'FIRST DROWNED
Remember me, Captain?

CAPTAIN CAT
You're Dancing Williams!

FIRST DROWNED
I lost my step in Nantucket.

SECOND DROWNED
Do you see me, Captain? the white bone talking? I'm
Tom-Fred the donkeyman . . . we shared the same girl
once . . . her name was Mrs. Probert . . .

WOMAN'S VOICE
Rosie Probert, thirty three Duck Lane. Come on up,
boys, I'm dead.

THIRD DROWNED
Hold me, Captain, I'm Jonah Jarvis, come to a bad
end, very enjoyable'.

And later, when Captain Cat recalls once more his youthful
lusts:

'ROSIE PROBERT
Knock twice, Jack,
At the door of my grave
And ask for Rosie.

CAPTAIN CAT
Rosie Probert.

ROSIE PROBERT
Remember her.
She is forgetting.
The earth which filled her mouth
Is vanishing from her.

Remember me.
I have forgotten you.
I am going into the darkness of the darkness for ever.
I have forgotten that I was ever born.

CHILD
Look. . . . Captain Cat is crying.

CAPTAIN CAT
Come back, come back,

FIRST VOICE
up the silences and echoes of the passages of the eternal night'.

The sense of loss is here so intensely and so unmercifully externalised to the listener that he must perforce suspend all criticism and weep with Captain Cat. Indeed, it is hard to be critical of *Under Milk Wood* for that very reason; the onrush of the play cajoles or bludgeons the critic into silence.

At the end of the play, when the ghosts are being laid, pity is assailed again:

'FIRST VOICE
Blind Captain Cat climbs into his bunk. Like a cat, he sees in the dark. Through the voyages of his tears he sails to see the dead.

CAPTAIN CAT
Dancing Williams!

FIRST DROWNED
Still dancing.

CAPTAIN CAT
Jonah Jarvis.

THIRD DROWNED
Still.

FIRST DROWNED
Curly Bevan's skull.

ROSIE PROBERT
Rosie, with God. She has forgotten dying.

FIRST VOICE
The dead come out in their Sunday best.

SECOND VOICE
Listen to the night breaking'.

Death moves everywhere under Milk Wood, not as a
cloaked and heroic Byronic Figure of Speech, but implicitly,
within man's simplest actions and his inevitable, ephemeral
condition; death, the other side of life's coin.

Polly Garter, the good-natured loose woman of the place,
('Me, Polly Garter, under the washing line, giving the
breast in the garden to my bonny new baby. Nothing
grows in our garden, only washing. And babies. And
where's their fathers live, my love? Over the hills and far
away. You're looking up at me now. I know what you're
thinking, you poor little milky creature. You're thinking,
you're no better than you should be, Polly, and that's good
enough for me. Oh, isn't life a terrible thing, thank God!'),
the easy consort of any man, is both the warm Goddess of
Fertility, the life-giver to so many, but also the fleshly
memorial to many who are now dead. They live on only

in her song, which, in Daniel Jones's plaintive and rather acidic setting, assaults the heart again and again, as it should be assaulted, without sentimentality, the wistful melody underpinning the poet's reminder of our immutable destiny:

> '*I loved a man whose name was Tom*
> *He was strong as a bear and two yards long*
> *I loved a man whose name was Dick*
> *He was big as a barrel and three feet thick*
> *And I loved a man whose name was Harry*
> *Six feet tall and sweet as a cherry*
> *But the one I loved best awake or asleep*
> *Was little Willy Wee and he's six feet deep*'.

And when Polly's song is counterpointed against the voices of children singing 'It was a Lover and his Lass', the effect is disastrous to Stoicism, for Thomas then shows us more forcefully than he was ever able to do before that life and love are an unending cycle, that the flower must bud and then die before it may be born again, that in accepting breath at all, man must learn to tolerate suffering and be prepared at last to go alone into the dark.

And that is the end of *Milk Wood* too, the darkness into which all these merry, sad, scheming, simple folk go. Thomas has brought them and himself to the end of a journey; now there is only night and the rustle of leaves:

'the suddenly wind-shaken wood springs awake for the second dark time this one Spring day'.

Epilogue

Reputations rise and fall, rise and fall, as incessantly as but much less accountably than barometers and tides. During his lifetime Dylan Thomas knew the uncertain glories of critical acclamation, and already generations both older and younger than his own have expressed pontifical doubts about him once more, some of them, the Elgin Marbles in their mouths, even wondering sadly whether he is entitled to the name *poet* at all.

In the most fustian grey decade of this century, such criticism is without authority, for he still stands, a natural, laughing little giant among a host of massively muscle-bound pygmies.

And even if, in a more balanced and final assessment, his small and sometimes galvanically wayward output does not measure up to the highest and absolute mark, there is still a quality in which no other writer has surpassed him, either in bulk or expression—that is, his sympathy with humanity.

Everywhere in his more lucid work there are pity, warmth and love; a knowledge and acceptance of frailty; an immeasurable tolerance.

For Dylan Thomas was not academically remote; he knew that he was involved in mankind; he had listened only too often to the voices of the river, and had long known that its bell tolled equally for him.

Analysis of a Poem

I T I S O N E of the fallacies of a certain sort of criticism that a poem should be capable of rendering itself in prose and of delivering itself of an unambiguous content, if it is to have the respect of the reader. Prime importance is placed on the degree to which each image and phase may be translated into everyday prose concepts.

It should be obvious (though it isn't, as can be seen by the correspondence often published in the literary journals on the occasion of a difficult poem) that a poem is itself and stands or falls by those canons of criticism which regard it as a poem, and not as an eccentric manner of presenting a prose-idea.

'What does it mean?' ask all adverse critics, from the man who shouldn't be reading poetry anyway, to those men who should long have stopped writing about it.

Therefore, I shall attempt here to show what a poem by Dylan Thomas *means*: that is, I shall translate it into a prose of my own. I do not know whether the poet would have approved of my rendering, or whether he would think I had missed the point of his poem completely. All I am saying is: 'This is what the poem means to me'. And I have chosen this particular poem, not because it is especially difficult, or representative even, but because, on at least three occasions, in the *Daily Express* and in private correspondence with me, James Agate has written it off as nonsense-verse. This is the poem from *The Map of Love:*

(January 1939)

Because the pleasure-bird whistles after the hot wires,
Shall the blind horse sing sweeter?
Convenient bird and beast lie lodged to suffer
The supper and knives of a mood.
In the sniffed and poured snow on the tip of the
         tongue of the year
That clouts the spittle like bubbles with broken
         rooms,
An enamoured man alone by the twigs of his eyes,
         two fires,
Camped in the dry-white shower of nerves and food,
Savours the lick of the times through a deadly
         wood of hair
In a wind that plucked a goose,
Nor ever, as the wild tongue breaks its tombs,
Rounds to look at the red, wagged root.
Because there stands, one story out of the bum city,
That frozen wife whose juices drift like a fixed sea
Secretly in statuary,
Shall I, struck on the hot and rocking street,
Not spin to stare at an old year
Toppling and burning in the muddle of towers and
         galleries
Like the mauled pictures of boys?
The salt person and the blasted place
I furnish with the meat of a fable;
If the dead starve, their stomachs turn to tumble
An upright man in the antipodes
Or spray-based and rock-chested sea:
Over the past table I repeat this present grace.

I would say that this poem means: 'Because a lark sings sweetly when it is blinded (a well-known practice), may we expect a horse to change its nature and to sing, if deprived of its eyes? This bird and this beast I take as examples, because they are convenient to my purpose; they are the food for thought on which I exercise the sharp knife of my present mood.

'Outside, lies the snow' ('sniffed and poured snow'—that is, sampled by smell and then poured out: a drug-reference, punning on 'snow', with a possible allusion to the isolating and silencing effects of actual snow, which also produces a world of fantasy by transforming the known world) 'in January, this first month of the year, the month which rests on the tip of the new year's tongue, when the weather is cold enough to make a man bubble at the mouth' (though it is possible that the line:

That clouts the spittle like bubbles with broken rooms

is a piece of verbal compulsion, almost of automatism).

'I, a lover, sit alone, warmed only by the small fires, the love, burning in my eyes' ('twigs' and 'eyes' is perhaps a back-reference to the 'hot wires' and the blind eyes of the lark), 'comforted by the food I have eaten, and protected from immediate and cruel realities by my imagination' (his 'nerves', covering him like a tent, a camp. The snow, also, is like a tent, and it is as white as a drug, aspirin, 'snow', which quietens the nerves. It is also like manna from Heaven, a food).

'So, sitting here alone, in the bitter weather, I consider the nature of life, and never once as I talk to myself of what life means, do I stop to consider what my tongue has said.

'Because, as we were taught in the false and deceiving town (in school?), Lot's wife was turned into a pillar of salt for looking back (she became salt of the sea, fixed, like a statue), shall I, in this chaotic town (which is as worn and jumbled as the cigarette-pictures which small boys carry about in their pockets), be afraid to look back, and to consider the past, the old year? I use Lot's wife and the ruined town as the elements of a fable, I clothe them with the substance of my beliefs'. (There is here, I imagine, more punning:

I furnish with the meat of a fable

i.e., furnish—fable (table)—meat on the table, leading on to 'starve', 'stomach', 'grace').

'What I wish to emphasise is that the past has great influence on the present, the dead on the living, even to the farthest corners of the earth.

'So, in this present time, I consider the past'.

One might further render down this explanation to something like this:

'It is impossible to rationalise life in terms of one image, or parable, or experience. Once must consider its chaos. Nor must one be afraid to turn round and regard the past, for only by understanding the past may we know the present'.

Or one could state it, in elementary verse, like this:

Can life be learned from one short word,
The image of a beast or bird?
No single key has yet set free
Man's coloured multiplicity.

The only comfort we may find
Is in the thoughtful ranging mind,
Which, knowing present cannot last,
Dares take its lesson from the past

By which time we have got well away from the words of the poem, and may wonder why the poet has taken so long to say so little! We may even come to believe in that criticism of Thomas's poems which says: 'they make great use of symbols, that they build up to the side of their subject and that the complete poem is then, so to speak, pointed at its subject' (C.B.S., *New Verse*, No. 23).

This is the most facile sort of criticism, but it is a constant danger, whenever one attempts the prose-explanation of a poem: particularly of poems as obscure as those of Dylan Thomas.

APPENDIX TWO

An Analysis of 'Light Breaks'

This poem is in regular stanza form, with a steady rhythm and occasional rime. Of the various levels of meaning it communicates, I take it that the basic level is a description of the state of existence; the theme is the process of living.

In the first stanza, the clue to the moment of existence which the poet is describing occurs in the 'warring images' of the last line. Since no flesh yet decks the bones, Thomas is probably referring, as he does elsewhere, to the period during or immediately after conception. Thus, the 'light' of prescience 'breaks' within the embryo, as the blood pushes through its veins like the tides of the ocean. The phrase, 'broken ghosts with glowworms in their heads', seems to be in apposition to 'The things of light', and to describe these intimations of consciousness or foreknowledge as they present themselves to the child in the womb. The contrast between the concrete and abstract nouns is great, although its success is precarious, and the reader is perhaps reminded of the poet's request to take his poems literally, seeking for no more detailed meaning. More generally, the particular word-order, 'where no sun shines', is established by three repetitions in the first stanza, to be repeated with diminishing frequency in the following stanzas. Its use is both formal and functional since it ties the poem together and permits a sharper conflict of images.

In the second stanza, the sexual symbolism of the 'candle

in the thighs' is clear, and that it 'warms youth and seed' makes sense. It also 'burns the seeds of age' in the sense of 'burn up', or even 'frustrate'. In the old or passionless, 'where no seed stirs', the poet says that 'the fruit of man unwrinkles in the stars'; that is, sublimation takes place and man's energies or thoughts turn heavenward or away from reality, perhaps toward religion. The word 'unwrinkles' is capable of an ironic sexual interpretation, as well as the following phrase, 'bright as a fig'; a fig may be shiny when ripe and young, or wrinkled when dry and old. The last varies the metaphor: 'where no wax is', where there is no flesh or vitality, 'the candle shows its hairs', the dead wick or the fleshless bone remains. This stanza contrasts the states of being young or old, virile or impotent.

In the third stanza, the statement that 'dawn breaks behind the eyes' may refer to the arrival of consciousness, presumably in the infant. The circulation of the blood in the body is referred to again and compared to the poles, tides, and winds of the earth. This image is clear, but the last three lines present a jumble of imagery. Any interpretation must hinge upon the meaning of 'gushers of the sky'. The connotations of rain, tears, and even oil-wells are reinforced in the following lines, although they are undeveloped. Further, the conceivable image of a gusher spouting to a divining rod lends itself to a sexual interpretation, while the word 'divining' may refer forward or backward and its use suggest a pun. The syntax is fluid, and the reader is inclined to equate 'gushers of the sky' simply with the processes of Nature and conclude that Thomas is saying that life goes on mingled with joy and sadness.

The fourth stanza, with its contrast of night and day, winter and spring, may best be interpreted in the light of the poet's belief that the soul should be stripped of darkness. The ball-in-socket image states the relationship; inside the

socket is likened to the pitch-black moon of the unknown
and the unconscious, the outside to the illumined bone of
truth or self-knowledge. The last three lines, as is the case
generally throughout the poem, are a variation of the
preceding idea. 'Where no cold is', or where the warmth
of knowledge exists, the 'skinning gales' or the process of
living ('skinning' because they flay or lay bare) loosen the
'winter's robe' or release the cold impulses of the unconscious. Again, a sexual interpretation of 'skinning gales' is
possible. The 'film of spring', or the prelude of self-knowledge, then becomes visible, existing just beyond the eyelids.
The contrasts in this stanza lend themselves to multiple
interpretations, and the poet is in danger of losing any
precise meaning in a welter of connotations.

The last stanza is perhaps the most elusive. The process
of self-exploration is described in terms of the visible or
conscious tips of buried thoughts which 'smell in the rain'.
The last phrase is striking in its context but ambiguous. It
may mean that the rain of self-analysis nurtures suppressed
thoughts as they break through the soil of the unconscious,
a meaning developed in the following lines, or more plaus-
ibly, that these beginnings of conscious realisation are evident
in the rain or process of existence. The next three lines, beginning with 'when logics die', are a little out of key, for
they appear to be an endorsement of the intuitive existence;
dispense with logic and the eye learns the 'secret of the soil',
while life becomes full or the 'blood jumps in the sun'. The
last line, however, is effective. In sudden contrast, Thomas
reminds us that above the 'waste allotments' of life, death
is hovering. 'Dawn', a word analogous to the words of light
with which the poem is teeming, comes to an end. Day may
follow, but it, too, will halt. We are born to die.

Marshall Stearns, from *'Transformation 3'* (Lindsay
Drummond).

Compound Words in Thomas's Early Poems

1. *Alliterative:*
   five-fathomed, sky-scraping, grave-gabbing, hemlock-headed, tree-tailed, tide-traced, sea-straw, sea-sawers, whale-weed, sea-struck, topsy-turvies, Tom-thumb, tell-tale, grave-groping, fair-formed, hard-held, sky-signs, come-a-cropper, hairy-heeled, windwell, scythe-sided, four-fruited, dog-dayed, man-melting, sea-sucked, to-morrow-treading.

2. *Sea- Compounds:*
   seawax, sea-blown, sea-faiths, sea-sucked, seafaring, sea-halved, seashores, water-clocks, tide-hoisted, sea-straw, tide-traced, sea-sawers, sea-ghost, whale-wed, sea-struck, sea-hatched, seawhirl, seaweedy, water-tower, sea-gut, water-lammed, seabed, sea-sucked, tide-tongued, ringed-sea.

3. *Negatives:*
   unangled, unriddle, unskated, ageless, riderless, unaccustomed, timelessly, headless, shapeless, unsucked, unborn, undead, unbuttoned, masterless, shadowless, unwrinkling.

4. *Triple Compounds:*
   come-a-cropper, hero-in-tomorrow, half-way-house, to-morrow-treading, bagpipe-breasted, seed-at-zero, god-

in-hero, man-in-seed, dry-as-paste, two-a-vein, bow-and-arrow, moon-and-midnight, Christ-cross-row.

5. *Eye- Compounds:*
Mothers-eyed, tallow-eyed, red-eyed, scythe-eyed, womb-eyed, salt-eyed, bull's-eye, eye-teeth, penny-eyed, stranger-eyes, bright-eyed, three-eyed.

6. *Number Compounds:*
two-gunned, four-stringed, twelve-winded, one-sided, half-blind, twin-boxed, three-coloured, five-fathomed, two-a-vein, four-fruited, four-winded, double-crossed, one-marrowed, one-dimensioned, two-framed, three-pointed, three-syllabled, half-tracked.

7. *Wise- Compounds:*
Altarwise, clockwise, Atlaswise, Venuswise, cockwise.

8. *Man- Compounds:*
Manshape, manseed, man-iron, manstring, man-waging, manwax, Abraham-man, yesman, fingerman, manshaped, man-melting, man-begetters.

9. *Scythe- Compounds:*
scythe-eyed, scythe-sided.

10. *Cross- Compounds:*
cross-bones, cross-stroked, cross-tree, Christ-cross-row.

11. *Clock- Compounds:*
clockwise, blowclock.

12. *Bone- Compounds:*
heartbone, boneyards, sawbones, bonerailed, cross-boned

13. *Heart- Compounds:*
heartbone, heartbreak, heart-shaped, sweethearting.

14. *Atlas- Compounds:*
Atlas-eater, Atlaswise.

15. *Moon- Compounds:*
moon-drawn, moon-turned, moon-and-midnight

16. *Grave- Compounds:*
graveward, grave-groping, grave-gabbing.
17. *Star- Compounds:*
star-flanked, polestar, star-gestured.
18. *Owl- Compounds:*
owl-light, owl-seed.
19. *Pin- Compounds:*
pin-legged, pin-hilled.
20. *Hand- Compounds:*
handprint, handmade, handsaw, handbell, spade-handed, country-handed, thumb-stained.
21. *Other Compounds:*
clayfellow, winding-sheets, year-hedged, hang-nail, Christward, planet-ducted, skull-foot, goblin-sucker, marrow-ladle, breast-deep, bread-sided, close-up, arc-lamped, sheath-decked, black-tongued, deadweed, Bible-leaved, wind-turned, bell-voiced, bird-papped, tear-drops, heaven-driven, rockbirds, foam-blue, spinning-wheels, steeple-jack, cock-on-a-dunghill, cell-stepped, fin-green, All-hallowed, shaping-time, outel-bowed, blood-red, air-drawn, warbearing, sand-bagged, sin-eater, vagueness, deadrock, windwell, night-time, rooftops, suncock, long-tailed, fly-lord, marrowroot, blacktongued, redhaired, hellborn, bloodred, lovebeds, muscling-in, raw-edged, crow's-foot, love-darkness, winding-footed, dark-vowelled, pickbrain, kissproof, spentout, 'planing-heeled, resuffered, cloud-tracking, time-faced.

Proper Names in Thomas's Early Poems

Biblical (24)	*Classical* (11)	*General* (17)
Gabriel	Caesar	(a) *Geographical*
Aaron	Venus	Cairo
Genesis	Odyssey	Asia
Exodus	Medusa	Nile
Jordan	Virgil	Glamorgan
Abaddon	Mermen	Wales
Adam	Siren	Capricorn
Eloi	Triton	and Cancer
Jacob	Neptune	Aran
Eve	Byzantine	Dead Sea
Pharaoh	Dolphin	Irish Sea
Mary (or Our Lady)		Sargasso
Jesu		(b) *Literary and*
Christ		*Mythological*
Jericho		Rip Van
Eden		Winkle
John		Jack Frost
Job		Hamlet
Abraham		Moby
Peter		Tom-thumb
Ishmael		Grail
Jonah		Mnetha
Lazarus		(c) Davy's Lamp
God		